Pearson's Canal Companion
CHESHIRE RING

Published by Central Waterways Supplies
Rugby - Tel/fax 01788 546692
email: sales@centralwaterways.co.uk
Copyright: Michael Pearson - all rights reserved
Eighth edition 2005   ISBN 0 9549116 0 1
Printed in Italy by Stige of Torino

tillerman

Locking up the Ribble Link, I fell in with three elderly ladies taking a short cut to their local library. Fell in, that is, in the sense that we got into conversation, and not - obviously -that all four of us were simultaneously immersed in the mulligatawnyesque waters of Savick Brook. The smallest, oldest and most loquacious of the trio (who I pictured once as a vivacious mill girl) confided that she had donated 'a ten bob note' to the laudable cause of connecting the Lancaster Canal to the rest of the inland waterways as long ago as 1957.

I don't suppose she could ever have imagined the link materialising in the way it has, but canal folk by their nature are music makers and dreamers of dreams, and as far as they are concerned nothing is ever an entirely lost cause. As I was putting this eighth edition of the *Cheshire Ring Canal Companion* together, word reached me that the Manchester, Bolton & Bury Canal was going to be restored. Goodness knows where we will put it, for this guide is already bursting at the seams; and we still haven't covered the Lancaster yet!

Such shortcomings notwithstanding, enjoy your journeys over these canals. They bring fresh perspectives to me whenever I visit them. I hope they'll prove just as

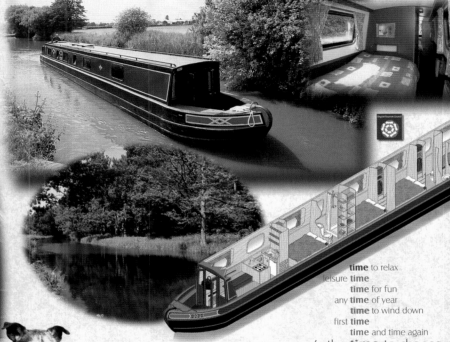

Booking a Holiday..?
Buying a Boat..? Own a Boat..?

Whether you are looking to hire a narrowboat for a holiday, buy one or already own one, you need look no further than Alvechurch.

With over 25 years experience of both operating the UK's finest fleet of holiday craft and building boats, you can be sure that we can help you with all you need to cruise the Great British Waterways. Now with 7 start locations giving access to almost the entire British canal network.

We also offer full marina services including repairs, breakdown, refit work, boat painting, brokerage service and boats for sale, moorings, diesel, gas, pumpouts and RYA Helmsman Training

Visit *Heart* of England
The Regional Tourist Board

HIRE CRAFT OPERATOR OF THE YEAR 2003
GOLD AWARD WINNER
in the Heart of England Excellence in Tourism Awards

ALVECHURCH
WATERWAY HOLIDAYS

Tel: 08708 35 25 25   Fax: 08708 35 25 55   Email: enquiries@alvechurch.com   Web: www.alvechurch.com
Alvechurch Boat Centres, Scarfield Wharf, Alvechurch, Worcestershire B48 7SQ

The
CHESHIRE
Ring

T HE Macclesfield and Trent & Mersey canals meet formally at Hall Green on the outskirts of Kidsgrove; though travellers who have made the journey up from Hardings Wood are entitled to feel already acquainted with "The Macc", as it is popularly known. The sequence of events which led to this anomaly is typical of the Trent & Mersey's paranoia in its dealings with potential rivals. Far from welcoming trade which the new Macclesfield Canal might bring in its wake, the T&M saw only a threat to its established link between Manchester and The Potteries via Middlewich and Preston Brook. Feeling that they would be in a stronger position if the Macclesfield was not able to gain access to their main line, they built a connecting canal out to meet the newcomer at HALL GREEN. Here, both companies regarded each other in mutual mistrust across a 'Checkpoint Charlie' of paired stop locks, paired lock-keeper's cottages, and paired stable blocks. Now, only one of the stop locks remains in use, and northbound boaters have a relaxing pound of nine miles in which to rest on their laurels before grappling with Bosley Locks.

Folly-topped MOW COP dominates the gritstone escarpment, rising to over a thousand feet, which runs parallel to the canal. The castellated ruin, known as Wilbraham's Folly, is typical of 18th century landscape enhancement and dates from 1754 when it was erected to be seen from Squire Wilbraham's Rode Hall, a couple of miles away on the Cheshire Plain. But Mow (pronounced to rhyme with cow) Cop's true claim to fame is that the first open air camp meeting of the Primitive Methodist Revivalists was held on its heights one Sunday morning in May 1807.

The smooth lawns of Ramsdell Hall (c1760) sweep down to the canal bank. Untypically ornate cast iron railings separate the towpath from a steep drop into the field below, so that the canal acts as a sort of ha-ha, or sunken wall, at the edge of the gardens. A mischievous image springs to mind of the gentry taking tea on the terrace and studiously ignoring the vulgar gaze of passing bargees - "Don't look, Daphne, don't look!"

A house of even greater antiquity can be glimpsed across rolling farmlands to the west, the incomparable Little Moreton Hall, one of England's greatest half-timbered buildings. Mow Cop & Scholar Green railway station closed in 1964 but was immortalised (along with a number of other stations with canal connections) by Flanders & Swann in their song *Slow Train*.

Public footpath from Church Lawton

By-road from Rode Heath

A34

Little Moreton Hall

Scholar Green

Kent Green

Watery Lane Aqueduct   mp

23

94   93   92   91   90   89   (88)   87   86   85   84   83   82   81   80

Hall Green Lock1ft 0ins

Crse of former colliery tramway

Heritage

70'

Ramsdell Hall

site of Mow Cop & Scholar Green rly sta

70'

Lockett's Tenement

By-roads to Mow Cop

By-roads to Mow Cop

Scholar Green   Map 1

Every May, several hundred runners gather close to Bridge 87 to participate in the 'Mow Cop Killer Mile' - a 'novelty' race that has now gained cult status. Every step of the route is uphill, culminating in a 1 in 3 section near the top. The winning time is normally in the region of 6 minutes 20 seconds, achieved by athletes capable of almost a four-minute mile on the track, which gives some idea of the severity of the course. Fancy following in their footsteps? Go on, the view from the summit stretches from The Potteries to the Mersey and is as breathtaking as the climb.

RISING SUN - adjacent to Bridge 87. Friendly pub within easy reach of the canal. Tel: 01782 776235. Also nearby is a Chinese-owned fish & chip shop.

Post office, newsagent and 'late shop' on the A34.

LITTLE MORETON HALL - twenty minutes walk from Bridge 85, 4 miles south-west of Congleton on A34. Tel: 01260 272018. Refreshments and NT shop. One of the most celebrated examples of a half-timbered house in England, Little Moreton Hall dates from the end of the 15th century. Top heavy, with leaning walls and sagging roofs, it seems like some vast, unstable doll's house.

Congleton   Map 2

Congleton has an unexpected zest about it, a level of activity which seems almost metropolitan to boaters, down from the cut with mud on their boots and a gauche unfamiliarity with road traffic. The best building in the town is the Town Hall, an imposing Flemish looking building which houses the Tourist Information Centre. Next door is the town's museum which celebrates its bear-baiting past, the former mayor who ordered the execution

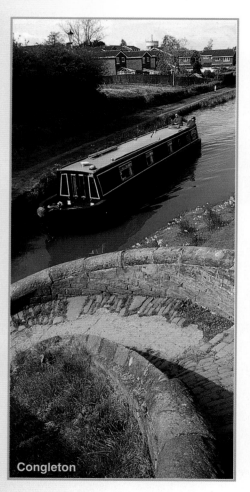

Congleton

of King Charles I, its former textile industries, and its connections with Dutch soldiery during the Second World War.

WHARF INN - adjacent Dog Lane Aqueduct. CAMRA recommended local offering home-made food and guest ales. Tel: 01260 272809.

RAILWAY INN - adjacent Bridge 75. Comfortable Bass pub, food (not Sundays) and pool. Tel: 01260 272527.

L'ENDROIT - Lawton Street. French restaurant. Tel: 01260 299548.

TASTE OF RAJ PREMIER - Lawton Street. Award-winning Indian restaurant. Tel: 01260 291800.

OATCAKES - Lawton Street. Fresh filled oatcakes and pikelets. Tel: 01260 298040.

Fish & chips and sandwich bar by Bridge 75.

Hightown offers a good selction of shops (Spar, bakery, delicatessen, post office and grocery) accessed via Bridge 75. The town centre is 10 to 15 minutes walk west of the canal, but there are bus connections - see below. Tuesdays and Saturdays are Market Days.

TOURIST INFORMATION CENTRE - Town Hall, High Street. Tel: 01260 271095. www.congletonarea.com

CONGLETON MUSUEM - Market Square. Tel: 01260 276360. Closed Mondays. Small admission charge. www.congletonmuseum.co.uk

BUSES - half-hourly Mon-Sat to/from Town Centre from stop adjacent to Dog Lane Aqueduct. Ditto hourly from stop adjacent to railway station and Bridge 75. Tel: 0870 608 2 608.

TRAINS - Virgin services to/from Stoke, Macclesfield and Manchester bi-hourly. A few peak-hour Northern services link Congleton with Macclesfield and Kidsgrove. Tel: 08457 484950.

TAXIS - Bear Town. Tel: 01260 291070.

NORTHBOUND, hills with a Pennine hardness about them begin to close in on the canal: southwards the landscape turns conversely softer as you head for the Midlands. CONGLETON'S canalside is semi-detached and suburban. Not before time its wharf and imposing warehouse have benefited from refurbishment. Oakes animal feedstuffs mill overlooks an unusual gathering of transport modes by Bridge 75. A high embankment pierced by small aqueducts carries the canal over the steep-sided valley of Shaw Brook. A branch of the North Staffordshire Railway once threaded the valley and its trackbed has become a popular public footpath. A rail/canal transhipment dock survives in water at Bridge 72 and can usefully be used as casual moorings by anyone wishing to fantasise that they've a cargo to swap with the ghost trains.

Whilst for much of its length the Macclesfield Canal travels along a roughly North-South axis, above Congleton it runs briefly East-West as it is forced to steer a course between the foot of The Cloud and the valley of the Dane. If you have energy to spare after tackling Bosley Locks, then an ascent of The Cloud is worth considering. This is best achieved from Bridge 61, taking the by-road past half-timbered Crossley Hall, over the railway, and then on for the best part of a mile, until you reach a crossroads from which a footpath sign beckons (fairly vertically it must be said) to the summit. When you get there, you'll be 1,126ft above sea level and over 700ft higher than the canal which snakes across the landscape below you to reach the foot of Bosley Locks whose chamber stones were quarried from The Cloud.

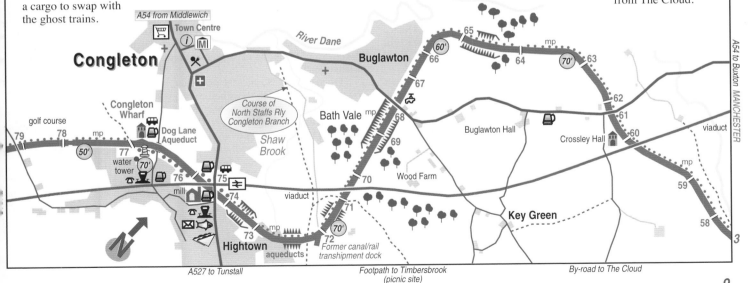

A54 from Middlewich

Town Centre

Congleton

River Dane

Buglawton

golf course

Congleton Wharf

Course of North Staffs Rly Congleton Branch

Bath Vale

Buglawton Hall

Crossley Hall

viaduct

A54 to Buxton MANCHESTER

Dog Lane Aqueduct

Shaw Brook

water tower

mill

Wood Farm

Key Green

viaduct

Hightown

aqueducts

Former canal/rail transhipment dock

A527 to Tunstall

Footpath to Timbersbrook (picnic site)

By-road to The Cloud

9

L OCKS on "The Macc" remind you of that old joke about waiting for a bus - you don't get one for ages and then they all come at once. The locks all come at BOSLEY - a dozen in a mile - and it is one of the most superbly engineered and magnificently located flights in the country; notably, for a narrow canal, in that both sets of gates to each stone chamber are mitred pairs. Once each chamber had a side pond, a water saving device which acted as a mini reservoir. When the lock emptied, half its contents would run into the side pond to be retained for half filling the chamber when it was next used. Theoretically this system halved the amount of water used by the flight. But perhaps British Waterways felt that operation of the locks in this manner was beyond the competence of amateur boat crews, because the side pond system was allowed to fall out of use some time ago.

At the foot of Bosley Locks the canal crosses the River Dane on an imposing stone aqueduct, best appreciated from the footpath which descends to the valley floor from Bridge 57. Blissfully peaceful and remote moorings are to be had below Lock 12. North of Bosley the canal, at its summit level of 518ft, traverses the foothills of the Peak District. Between bridges 49 and 50 it occupies a shelf above a steeply sided valley reminiscent of a West Country combe. The woods are filled with chattering jays, whilst in summer the air is heavy with the scent of wild garlic.

Bridge 49 is an electrically operated swing bridge for which boaters will need a BW Yale key to gain access to the control panel. Be methodical in following the instructions and don't panic if you suddenly find a queue of motorists delayed by your boat's snail-like passage through the bridge. For although it is only a minor road which is carried across the canal, it can be surprisingly busy at times, especially during the school run when Cheshire's womenfolk take to the roads in their huge 4X4 vehicles which appear better suited to delivering aid parcels to remote villages in the Third World.

OAKGROVE is no more than a spattering of houses on the Leek-Macclesfield Grand Prix race track, though the Fool's Nook is a comfortable country inn. By swing-bridge No.47 (which boaters should ensure is returned to closed position after use), a gnarled wood marks the perimeter of Danes Moss, a peat bog reminiscent of Whixall Moss on the Llangollen Canal.

Opened in 1831, the Macclesfield Canal remained independently owned for just fifteen years before being acquired by a constituent of what was to become the Great Central Railway. The ubiquitous Thomas Telford surveyed it, but, being a busy man, had little to do with its construction.

STOKE

viaduct
River Dane

Course of Churnet Valley Railway

2

57
aqueduct

Staffs

site of old ng rly wharf

Cheshire

55   5-2
6
Bosley Locks
8/7 No.s 1-12 110ft
12   56
11-9

Bosley Feeder

54   1
53

Bosley Services

BT Tower

Jodrell Bank
mp

52

51
mp
50

49
60'

Fools Nook

Oakgrove

Danes Moss

47   46
site of bone works
(48)

48A
mp

Lyme Green

Sutton Reservoir

A523 to Leek   A54 to Buxton

*T*HE Macclesfield Canal looks down over the slate rooftops and terracotta chimney pots of the town which gave it its name. Here was the Company's headquarters and their Brook Street Wharf, overlooked by a handsome mill which once belonged to Hovis the breadmakers. That the canal played an important part in transport to and from the mill can be seen from the arched loading bay at water level. Hovis transferred their milling activities to Trafford Park, Manchester, where ships could import grain and wheat direct to their door, but they still used this mill as a print works for their packaging and publicity material. By Bridge 38 stands an old canal toll house.

A cutting of high-sided stone retaining walls frames the canal's southern approach to Macclesfield. Perhaps Crossley, the canal's engineer, was already aware of construction techniques on the Liverpool & Manchester Railway, for there is a strong 'railway' character to this cutting. At GURNETT another cutting of this kind lies just north of an aqueduct which carries the canal above the road to Sutton Lane Ends and the River Bollin. West of here Tegg's Nose dominates the view, a former gritstone quarry which has become a country park in its retirement.

Dry-stone walls criss-cross little fields climbing bravely up the hillsides, with here and there a knotty tentacle of stone terrace housing. This is Tunnicliffe Country. The famous wildlife artist was born at nearby Langley in 1901. Though best known as an illustrator of other author's works - Henry Williamson's *Tarka the Otter* for example - Charles Tunnicliffe also wrote and illustrated his own nature diaries, a number of which feature local scenes such as the canal reservoir at Bosley.

The Pennine Hills beckon enticingly from Bridge 33, but, travelling northwards, Macclesfield is difficult to shake off completely, because Hurdsfield's industrial estate parallels the canal for much of the way to Bollington, but the canal, as so often seems to be the case, remains aloof and largely quiet and unspoilt. The towpath changes sides at Bridge 29, a typically attractive Macclesfield roving bridge. To the north-east the wooded slopes of Kerridge Hill dominate the skyline, topped by a sugarloaf-shaped stone monument. Built to commemorate the Battle of Waterloo, it is known to all and sundry as 'White Nancy'. It is hereabouts that those travelling anti-clockwise around the Cheshire Ring begin to feel well and truly under the influence of The North. Time to surreptitiously slip on a cloth cap and clogs, to drop your voice several tones, to cease smiling, and to greet other canal users with a curt "Ey-up" before wiping your nose on your sleeve and spitting into t' cut.

Oakgrove
Map 3

FOOLS NOOK - comfortable country inn on A523 adjacent to swing bridge No.49. Boddingtons and food. Tel: 01260 252254.

GAWSWORTH HALL - two miles west of Bridge 49. Half-timbered house of considerable charm open to the public at Easter and from May to September. Concerts and special events. Tel: 01260 223456 www.gawsworthhall.com

Macclesfield
Map 4

Macclesfield has some charming nooks and crannies, and some interesting museums which make it worth a semi-colon in the punctuation of any canal itinerary. Follow Buxton Road down from Bridge 37, past Arighi Bianci's fabulously ornate furniture store, pass under the railway and you'll find yourself in Waters Green, where Wesley preached and which Tunnicliffe painted. Cobbled Church Street leads steeply up to the town centre and the fine, Greek Revival style Town Hall, adjoining which, the Tourist Information Office makes an excellent point of departure for further exploration of this old silk making town.

PUSS IN BOOTS - canalside Bridge 37. Popular stone pub overlooking canal basin. Bar meals available. Tel: 01625 423261.

WATERS GREEN TAVERN - Waters Green. CAMRA recommended town pub offering Taylor's Landlord and guest beers with food at lunchtime. Tel: 01625 422653.

THE CHESHIRE GAP - 87 Mill Street. Nice deli/bakery/cafe. Tel: 01625 425806.

PAPPAGALLO - Mill Street. Excellent Italian restaurant. Tel: 01625 619477.

LA CANTINA - Mill Street. Tapas bar. Tel: 01625 439999.

CHRISTINE'S SANDWICH SHOP - adjacent Bridge 37. Tel: 01625 410888.

Full facilities in the town centre 10 minutes walk from the canal. Indoor market Mon-Sat, outdoor market Tue, Fri & Sat. CHESHIRE GAP on Mill Street is an excellent delicatessen, whilst nearby a fishmongers called CHESHIRE FISH stands appropriately enough on Roe Street.

TOURIST INFORMATION - Town Hall, Market Street Tel: 01625 504114. www.macclesfield.gov.uk

SILK MUSEUM & PARADISE MILL - Park Lane. Tel: 01625 612045. Paradise Mill once housed a silk handloom weaving business.

HERITAGE CENTRE - Roe Street. Tel: 01625 613210. The story of silk and its development within Macclesfield. Plus local history. Shop and cafe.

WEST PARK MUSEUM - Prestbury Road. Tel: 01625 619831. Fine and decorative arts, including the work of C. F. Tunnicliffe.

BUSES - bus station on Sunderland Street adjacent to rail station. Tel: 0870 608 2 608.

TRAINS - 5 minutes downhill from Bridge 37. Virgin and Northern services. Frequent connections with Manchester and Stoke. Through trains to/ from London. Tel: 08457 484950.

TAXIS - Silvertown. Tel: 01625 611333.

Bollington
Map 5

The last cotton mill ceased spinning in 1960 and now Bollington is as spick and span and as pretty as any hill town in Umbria - if you are going to 'drop anchor' anywhere on 'The Macc' this is the place to do so!

BRISCOLA - Palmerston Street. Atmospheric and deservedly popular Italian restaurant. Tel: 01625 573898.

BEASDALES - High Street. Tel: 01625 575058. Fine dining.

Lots of nice individual shops whose owners seem genuinely interested in visitors 'off the cut': facilities include post office, newsagent, wine shop, launderette, chemist and small MACE supermarket (with cash machine).

BUSES - frequent services to/from Macclesfield plus a service via Adlington to Stockport useful for towpathers. Tel: 0870 608 2 608.

Higher Poynton
Map 6

COFFEE TAVERN - cosy cafe dating back as far as 1876 when it was opened by Lord Vernon, owner of the Poynton area coal mines, as a temperance alternative to the adjacent pub. Good choice of food including Hollands Pies. Tel: 01625 874315.

BOARS HEAD - friendly Boddingtons pub offering a good choice of food. Tel: 01625 878325.

TRADING POST - canalside dealer in boating accessories (fenders, gas, oil etc) plus canalia,refreshments and confectionery. Tel: 01625 872277 www.canaltradingpost.com

NELSON PIT VISITOR CENTRE - two minutes walk from Bridge 15. Interesting displays and interpretive material relating to Higher Poynton's coal mining past and the railway origins of the Middlewood Way. Local walks leaflets and toilet facilities. For further details contact Macclesfield Leisure Services on 01625 504509.

ANSON ENGINE MUSEUM - five minutes walk from Bridge 15. Delightful small museum celebrating the internal combustion engine, located on the site of Anson Pit, closed in 1926. Irresistible Xanadu of fabled names - Gardner, Ruston, Hornsby, Tangye, National, Mirrlees etc etc. Open Fri, Sat, Sun and Bank Hols, April to October, 10am-5pm. Tel: 01625 874426.

PROOF, if proof were needed, that you are high up in the foothills of the Pennine backbone of England, lies less than a mile from Bridge 17. It is the western boundary of the Peak District National Park, marked so distinctly on the Ordnance Survey map, as if there were some sudden, fundamental alteration to the character of the landscape. But, in any case, there is plenty of circumstantial evidence that you are "Up North" now. Not least in the dignified, post-industrial mills of BOLLINGTON. With their flamboyant architectural embellishments they look more like baronial country seats, which is probably exactly what their owners had in mind. In those days pride came before profit margins. The canal soars above Bollington on a high, stone laid embankment pierced by a lofty aqueduct which acts like a sort of 19th century portcullis to this atmospheric mill town. It would be nice to see the vegetation cleared to reveal the embankment in its raw, stone laid state.

The canal traveller is treated to some tremendous views.

Eastwards the Pennine escarpment keeps inspirational company with the canal. Westwards, Alderley Edge ends abruptly on the Cheshire Plain. On a clear day Stockport and Manchester, are well defined on the horizon, whilst nearer at hand is Woodford Aerodrome. Two famous aircraft designs made their inaugural flights from here: the Lancaster bomber in 1941 and the Shackleton reconnaissance plane eight years later.

In a perfect world, all towpaths would be well surfaced and all dismantled railways public rights of way. Macclesfield Borough Council embraced this ideal back in 1985, refurbishing some 15 miles of towpath within their area, and establishing the "Middlewood Way", an 11 mile route for walkers, horse riders and cyclists from the remains of the old Macclesfield to Marple railway closed in 1970. The result is an interlinking network of recreational routes - 'Pathways from the Past', as the promotional leaflets put it - which is popular with locals and visitors alike, though there are signs, twenty years on, that the towpath in particular is in need of remedial work to return it to the high standard originally attained. Nature, as all gardeners know only too well, is an unforgiving taskmaster.

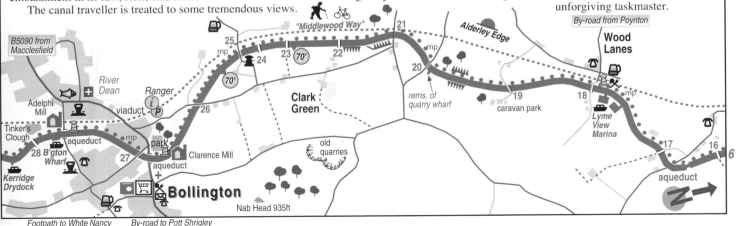

Goyt Mill, near Marple

AFTER the exciting passage above the rooftops of Bollington, or the long ascent of Marple Locks, this stretch of canal permits a certain amount of relaxation; yet never becomes tedious, for half Cheshire is spread before you, a turquoise sea lapping on the distant shore of Wales.

Goyt Mill, by Bridge 3, is one of the most impressive you'll encounter on the Cheshire Ring. Built early in the century - predominantly of red brick with cream lining - it spun cotton imported through Manchester Docks and brought here by canal. Spinning ceased in the Sixties as the British textile industry declined in the face of Far Eastern competition. But like many of these stately Northern mills, the huge building's echoing galleries now house an exotic variety of small businesses. According to some sources it was to Goyt mill that the last commercial traffic on the Macclesfield Canal - coal from Stoke-on-Trent - survived until 1957.

If it wasn't cotton it was coal. Between the mills of Bollington and Marple "The Macc" traverses a former mining area. Clues abound, but encroaching nature has rendered most of them subtle. Much activity centred on MOUNT VERNON WHARF where a fleet of coal carrying narrowboats was maintained. An interpretive board illustrates what the wharf would have looked like in its heyday. Nowadays the basins are busy with private pleasure craft. Leisure boating is nothing new to the Macclesfield Canal. Its beauty was already appreciated by the Second World War when the North Cheshire Cruising Club (whose journal was endearingly known as "The Ditchcrawler") was established on an old coal loading arm at HIGH LANE. A peculiarity, then as now, was the use of boathouses - the aquatic equivalent of a lock-up garage - one of which remains on the main line at Marple (Map 7).

South of Bridge 15 the canal widens into a shallow pool, probably brought about by a burst. Presumably it was cheaper to pay out compensation to the farmer than go to the trouble of repairing the canal bank. The bridges in this former colliery area differ in design from the graceful stone arches one generally associates with the Macclesfield Canal. They are flat decked and designed to be easily raised in the event of subsidence brought about by mining.

Canalside the emphasis may have been on trade, but towards the eastern horizon the moors rise up in handsome waves. The tower visible in the middle distance is known as "The Cage" and is thought to have been erected in Elizabethan times as a vantage point from which to watch the hunting of deer. Deer lead a less wild (but who is to say better?) existence now at a venison farm bordering the canal by Bridge 7.

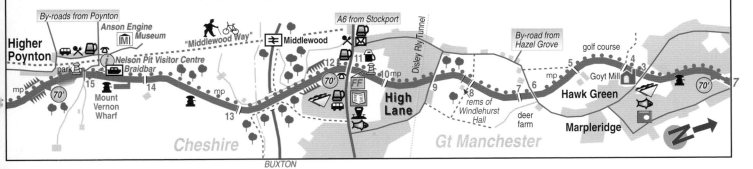

MARPLE is the meeting place of the Macclesfield and Peak Forest canals. It's a superbly photogenic junction, abounding in great sweeps of stonework and cobbles, about which there's a well kept air of confidence in accord with its strategic position on the Cheshire Ring. There is so much to see that it is one of those locations which attracts more than its fair share of gongoozlers. Apart from the seemingly endless fascination locks hold for people who don't actually have to operate them, one of the main attractions is the Macclesfield Company's perishable goods warehouse, a durable stone building with an arched loading bay adjoining a former stop lock and a functionally stylish roving bridge which enabled horses to haul boats through the junction without the need to unhitch the towing rope. Nearby, overlooking the top lock, is a toll house displaying a plaque commemorating the reopening of the Peak Forest Canal in 1974. On the opposite bank of the canal a sturdy stone house was once part of James Jinks's boatbuilding yard. A former drydock has been transformed into a sunken garden. It became disused in the Thirties, the story being that it leaked so badly that Mrs Jinks's cellar was flooded every time a boat entered or left the dock. Adjoining the old boatyard, below an arm now used for moorings, is a bank of limekilns which have about them the look of medieval ruins. It is thought that Samuel Oldknow, main promoter of the Peak Forest Canal, and a man who had his finger

in every money-spinning pie between Manchester and Stockport, had the kilns built like this to romanticise the view from his house across the valley.

Lower Peak Forest Canal

The Peak Forest Canal is the senior partner at Marple, predating the Macclesfield by thirty years. Engineered by Benjamin Outram, it was opened between Bugsworth and Ashton-under-Lyne in 1800, primarily for the carriage of limestone quarried in the Derbyshire hills. As construction of the canal forged ahead, the company ran into what we would now call cash-flow problems. Outram, already experienced in the construction of tramways, recommended that the planned flight of locks at Marple be replaced by a tramway. However, from the outset, trade was so successful that, within four years,

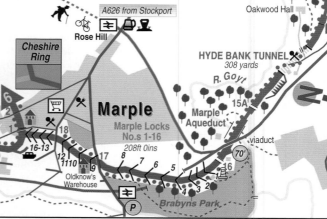

*Figures relate to Cheshire Ring, allow 45 mins for Upper Peak Forest.

16

the flight was built as originally intended.

MARPLE LOCKS are enormously satisfying for the spectator and participant alike; though the former may have more energy to explore their elusive and engaging details: like the horizontal rope roller on the parapet of Bridge 17. But no-one's going to miss Oldknow's warehouse above Lock 9, a stunningly handsome, three storey stone structure now housing a suite of enviable offices. Oldknow had a mill at Mellor, and bales of finished cotton were brought here by road for storage before onward transit along the canal.

Bridge 18 is known as Posset Bridge, apparently because Oldknow promised the navvies a posset of ale apiece if they finished the bridge on schedule. History records that they did! The bridge incorporates separate horse and foot tunnels and, on the offside, an arch indicates a former arm to the foot of the limekilns. Another short arm left the canal at this point and led to Hollins Mill. Green's coal boats traded here as late as 1959, one of the last commercial traffics on the canal. The top four chambers of the flight must be unique in their setting alongside the neat front gardens of a street of suburban villas. A series of extended side ponds have been transformed into duck-busy backwaters.

At the foot of the flight the canal is overlooked by lush Brabyns Park. Peaceful moorings are available and constitute a deeply desirable location in which to recover from the exertions of the sixteen locks - or to prepare yourself mentally for the ascent. As if all this excitement wasn't enough, another Peak Forest highlight lies - quite literally - just around the corner. Undoubtedly the canal's most dramatic gesture, the splendid MARPLE AQUEDUCT carries the waterway almost a hundred feet across a steeply wooded ravine carved by the impatient River Goyt. Alongside, in a juxtaposition reminiscent of Chirk on the Llangollen Canal, stands an even loftier railway viaduct. It is from here, perhaps aboard a comparatively slow-moving Manchester to Marple Rose Hill train, that an excellent view of the aqueduct is to be enjoyed. Alternatively, from its northern end, a stepped path - on which you may have to come to terms with vertigo - leads precipitously down through the trees to offer another superb view of the aqueduct, this time allowing appreciation of its unusual cylindrical hollowed sections, built in such fashion to lessen the weight of masonry resting on the support piers.

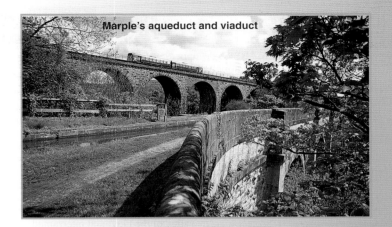

Marple's aqueduct and viaduct

Travelling in a north-westerly direction, you pass through quiet woodlands before penetrating the murky depths of HYDE BANK TUNNEL. Once there was another tunnel at Rose Hill where Bridge 15A spans a narrow cutting. Between here and Hyde Bank, the towpath is chaperoned by huge stone buttresses, built to shore up the canal and prevent it from bursting into the foaming waters of the Goyt far below. There is no towpath through Hyde Bank Tunnel but walkers and cyclists may proceed by way of the old horsepath across the top, itself bridged by the carriageway to Oakwood Hall. Hyde Bank Farm Tea Room is an added attraction. During the First World War Oakwood cotton mill was used for the manufacture of margarine; nowadays it is occupied by a packaging firm. Far down below the level of the canal, Chadkirk Chapel has a history dating dating back to the 7th Century and can be reached on foot from the aqueduct.

Still defiantly rural, the Peak Forest Canal continues to offer superb views north to the high fells that dominate the skyline. How inviting they look, how tempting it is to moor the boat and head off for a few hours hiking. Soon enough, however, the canal enters a shallow cutting and then the houses of Romiley - mostly with well tended gardens - begin to spill down to the water's edge.

SOUTH of MARPLE the upper level of the Peak Forest Canal journeys exhilaratingly through a vigorous landscape of fells, wind-bent woods, lonely stone cottages, railway viaducts and colossal mills, to its twin termini: at WHALEY BRIDGE, where it once connected with the celebrated Cromford & High Peak Railway, and the recently re-watered BUGSWORTH. Ironically, it was this upper section which lost its trade after Bugsworth Basin was abandoned in the Twenties. That it stayed open was due to the location of two reservoirs above Whaley Bridge. Nowadays the canal is busy with pleasure boats and there are many private moorings. Such popularity isn't hard to fathom, for this is a particularly beautiful canal in an austere, Northern mould. Zig-zagging round its shapely escarpment above the valley of the Goyt and interrupted by the novelty of (windlass-operated) lift and swing bridges, canallers are blessed with a sense of privilege to be seeing the world from such an attractive angle.

New Mills NEWTOWN is the largest settlement encountered by the Upper Peak Forest Canal. Here, in premises adapted from an old canalside mill, is Swizzles-Matlows confectionery works, purveyor of sherberty smells and origin of all the sticky substances you find abandoned in your children's pockets. Beyond the busy boatyard the canal arcs around the hillside to reveal superb views of Kinder Scout - at 2,088 ft, the local Everest and highest point in Derbyshire. The marina at FURNESS VALE creates regular tidal waves of pleasure craft. Raised above the level of the canal, trains to Buxton rattle by at hourly intervals; the signal box retains its London Midland Region 1950s style enamel nameplate. On the opposite side of the valley another railway carries long trains of locally quarried limestone, the modern equivalent of the narrowboats which once carried the same commodity so successfully on the canal.

A pair of concrete road bridges introduces the junction of the original main line to Bugsworth Basin and the branch to Whaley Bridge; boat horses gained access to the latter via a tunnel.

Map labels

BUXTON

A5002 from Buxton
Toddbrook Res.

WHALEY BRIDGE

Whaley Bridge

70'

P

wc

Canal Basin

Tesco aqueduct

Bridgemont

Bothomes Hall (ruin)

Bugsworth Basins

sewage works

34

33

32

31

30

29

28

27

26

25

SHEFFIELD A6 from Buxton

N

Gowhole

Furness Vale Marina

Furness Vale

Newtown

New Mills Marina
Anglo Welsh

70'

70'

confectionery works

River Goyt

viaduct

Derbyshire

Cheshire

A6

Dandy Cock

Disley

Hague Bar

B6101

By-road to Chinley

By-road to New Mills

New Mills (5 mins)

An aqueduct carries the main line over the Goyt then it passes beneath the A6 before curving round to Bugsworth Basin. The Inland Waterways Protection Society may sound like some sort of boaters' mafia, but what they really are is a small, dedicated group of enthusiasts who have painstakingly restored BUGSWORTH BASINS to something approaching the glory of their commercial heyday. The tireless efforts of the IWPS came to fruition with reopening of the basins in 1999. Unfortunately this proved a false dawn, and leakage brought about an abrupt closure of the basins to boating traffic, a hiatus lasting half a dozen years. Happily, however, the complex reopened for the second time at Easter, 2005. The event was marked by the departure of a horse-drawn narrowboat loaded with 16 tons of crushed limestone bound for Guide Bridge.

Bugsworth today enjoys Ancient Monument status and what the IWPS has achieved amounts to the successful excavation of an archaeological site of considerable importance. The complex comprises a series of transhipment arms and basins which radiate from a gauging stop overlooked by a wharfinger's house and canal office. A six mile tramway descended from the limestone quarries of Dove Holes. Loaded wagons ran down to Bugsworth by gravity, whilst empty ones were horse-drawn back. These trains were known as 'gangs', and often totalled twenty wagons at a time under the control - if that's not too precise a term - of a brakeman and his 'nipper', or youthful assistant; both of whom somewhat perilously rode the leading wagon. It comes as no surprise to learn that derailments were not exactly an unknown phenomenon on the rudimentary L shaped track. At Chapel-en-le-Frith there was an inclined plane which operated on the principle that empty wagons were hauled upwards by the weight of loaded ones travelling downhill. In the heyday of the basins perhaps twenty narrowboats a day would leave Bugsworth laden with limestone for Lancashire's burgeoning industries. The tramway ceased operating in the 1920s, though one of its wagons has found its way into the National Railway Museum at York.

Meanwhile, back on the 'branch' to WHALEY BRIDGE, yet more private moorings signal the approach to this compact Derbyshire town. Shaded by woodlands, the canal runs parallel to the old, now by-passed A6 before terminating in a small, triangular basin dominated by a sizeable, stone-built, transhipment shed. An arm enters an archway in the centre of this handsome structure whilst, in the past, railway tracks were accommodated on either side to facilitate loading and unloading in sheltered conditions. Whereas the link at Bugsworth was by way of a fairly primitive tramway, the railway connection at Whaley Bridge, dating from 1831, was of a more sophisticated design. The Cromford & High Peak climbed right across the Peak District to link with the Cromford Canal, 33 miles to the south. Tantalisingly, the route was originally surveyed for the construction of a canal, but the Railway Age caught up with these heroic, not to say romantic proposals; more's the pity, when you contemplate what could have been one of Britain's most beautiful inland waterways.

For your part, you can stretch your legs along the course of the railway's steep incline which runs to the rear of the town's main street, and contemplate the profit and loss of historical chance. Canal termini are apt to have this effect on you, as if somehow mirroring life's own wasted opportunities. And where do we go from here, you ask? By train to Buxton perhaps, or simply wend your way back along the gorgeous Peak Forest Canal, but not too quickly ...

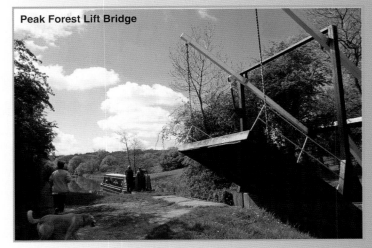

Peak Forest Lift Bridge

Marple

Subtract the canal, and its setting on the cusp of the moors, and Marple would amount to little more than a pleasant suburban annex of Stockport. That said, Marple's position on the 'Cheshire Ring' makes it a popular overnight mooring point and the town has some of the handiest and best facilities on this side of the circuit. Christopher Isherwood, author of *Goodbye Berlin* - from which the musical *Cabaret* was derived - was born here.

MARPLE WINE BAR - Stockport Road. Tel: 0161 427 1200. Wine bar and Spanish restaurant open daily 10am-11pm.
DOLCE VITA - Stockport Road. Tel: 0161 449 0648. Italian restaurant adjacent Bridge 18.
THE EDGE - Stockport Road. Fine cooking adjoining Bridge 18. Tel: 0161 427 0018.
HYDE BANK TEA ROOM - above Hyde Bank Tunnel. Tel: 0161 430 3582. Open Tue-Sun, 11am-5pm. Handsome barn conversion integral to 17th century working dairy farm. Coffees, lunches, teas. Fresh milk shakes!

Good shopping centre within easy reach of bridges 2 or 18, though some early closing on Wednesdays.

BUSES - frequent services to/from Stockport which is an interesting town in its own right. Tel: 0161 228 7811.
TRAINS - station just down hill from Bridge 17. Services to/from Manchester, Romiley, Guide Bridge, New Mills etc. Tel: 08457 484950. Rose Hill station, just over half a mile west of the town centre, is the terminus of an hourly service from Manchester, but it also marks the northern end of the Middlewood Way (converted from its abandoned trackbed after closure in 1970) and has thus much potential for walkers.

Newtown

A 19th century textile-based expansion of the North Derbyshire town of New Mills. Handy shops and a good fish & chip cafe. Station and pub. New Mills itself is a worthwhile quarter of an hour away on foot. Here, a heritage centre (open daily ex Mon - Tel: 01663 746904) interprets local history and there's a dramatic trail along the rivers Goyt and Sett.

Whaley Bridge

Disley

Likeable village, even if it's hard to cross the A6 in one piece. Nice walk to reach it along the lane from Bridge 25. Facilities include a Co-op, good butchers and bakers, pharmacy, off-licence, and a couple of banks. Good choice of eating places, including an Italian restaurant called CONTI (Tel: 01663 765400) and the DANDY COCK INN (Tel: 01663 766016), plus Chinese and Balti take-aways. Rail services to Manchester and Whaley Bridge.

Whaley Bridge

A charming little Derbyshire town sheltering under the moors of Axe Edge. Make the canal terminus a convenient excuse to explore the surrounding countryside. Go up and see the reservoirs in the Goyt Valley, flooded after the First World War.

SHEPHERD'S ARMS - Old Road. Tel: 01663 732840. Splendid whitewashed pub just a few hundred yards south of the basin close to the course of the former C&HP Railway (whose tracks are still to be seen on a nearby bow-sprung girder bridge across the river). Stone-flagged floor and unspoilt within.
NO. 29 looks like a nice little restaurant - Tel: 01663 734998.
TEAZEL'S - Canal Street. Cafe/bistro adjacent to basin. 9.30am-4pm ex Weds, plus Fri & Sat evenings for dinners. Tel: 01663 719200.
VILLAGE FRYER - good fish & chips on Canal Street. Tel: 01663 732902.

Plenty of small characterful shops where they are eager to pass the time of day with visiting canallers. Tesco supermarket handily placed for canallers close to the junction with the Bugsworth Arm.

TRAINS - local service to/from Buxton (a worthwhile destination for an excursion ashore) Stockport and Manchester with stops at Furness Vale, Newtown and Disley. Tel: 08457 484950.

Buxworth (Bugsworth)

NAVIGATION INN - adjacent Bugsworth Basin. Tel: 01663 732072. A fine old stone pub which once belonged to the Coronation Street stalwart, Pat Phoenix, alias 'Elsie Tanner'. Cosy atmosphere and canalia. Bar or restaurant food. Accommodation also.

*I*F it is the Goyt which shapes the course of the 'upper' Peak Forest Canal, then it is the Tame which influences the 'lower' level. The two rivers meet at Stockport and are known democratically thereafter as the Mersey; under which alias Cheshire Ring travellers encounter their waters again near Sale. Hereabouts the Tame Valley is less wild, more urbanised than the Goyt above Marple. In common with all these dashing Pennine torrents, the Tame's inherent power proved a boon to 18th century millowners before steam power took over. Sometimes the location of industry is an accident of history, more often than not there are cogent reasons for specific areas being closely associated with a particular activity. The manufacture of cotton goods established itself on this side of the Pennines because the climate was one of high humidity; because the local watercourses provided both power for the looms and soft water for washing and dyeing; because coal was at hand with the advent of steam; because there was sufficient population to provide the workforce; and finally because the proximity of the Mersey ports gave access to world markets. Like a pair of worn out bloomers, the bottom fell out of the cotton industry as man-made fibres became more fashionable and less expensive to produce. Furthermore, it became apparent that all but the top strata of British society could dress itself more efficiently in garments manufactured in the sweat shops of the Far East. So the mills were made redundant. Laid up like obsolete oil tankers on a Cornish tidal creek. The maritime analogy is apt. Like ships the mills bore proud names. They lay, chimneys belching smoke, in the folds of the landscape like ocean going vessels in a swell. Whilst in their galleries hundreds of human beings once toiled 'below deck' to earn a meagre living.

Although the canal is predominantly urban, it is never suffocated, being, on the contrary, misleadingly but convincingly rural; barely acknowledging the proximity of Romiley and Hyde, and managing to maintain a level of interest which doesn't pall. Hyde, these days, is difficult not to associate with Harold Shipman, but another Harold, the artist Harry Rutherford (1903-1985), has left the town a better legacy, not least his lovely painting of Hyde Market in 1948, called *Northern Saturday*.

By Bridge 8 little remains of Gee X Mill, still less of the eponymous trolleybus terminus at Gee Cross, outpost of the Manchester system, a lengthy eight mile run from Piccadilly. Long trains of containerised rubbish cross the railway bridge beside the northern portal of Woodley Tunnel. They're bound for Scunthorpe where Manchester's excess waste is buried in a big hole in the ground!

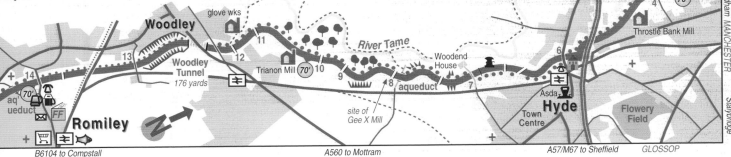

PORTLAND BASIN is one of the pivotal points of the Cheshire Ring. Three canal routes meet here amidst a backdrop of textile mills, and it would be hard to overstate the appeal of this location, architecturally or atmospherically. Astonishing, then, to recall that forty years ago all these canals were abandoned! Both the Ashton and Peak Forest canals were pronounced 'brain dead' during the Sixties and it took a canal enthusiasts' crusade to lobby authority to revive these waterways and to provide the muscle at the mucky end of their proposals. The Ashton and Peak Forest canals were reopened in 1974, but only after tens of thousands of voluntary man hours had been devoted to retrieving detritus from the beds of the canals.

Resurrection of the Huddersfield Canal (which actually meets the Ashton at Ashton Old Wharf half a mile east of Portland Basin) took somewhat longer, but now, following its complete re-opening in 2001, it is once more fully navigable all the way across the Pennines to Yorkshire - a remarkable achievement covered in our Pennine Waters Canal Companion.

The Peak Forest Canal

The Peak Forest Canal makes an acrobatic entrance into PORTLAND BASIN, hurling itself across the Tame on a substantial stone aqueduct provided by the Ashton Canal Company in anticipation of the opening of the route from Marple. A particularly handsome roving bridge, also of stone, spans the junction, framing a warehouse converted to house the Portland Basin Museum. Between here and Hyde the Peak Forest Canal's course is most notable for the rich aromas emanating from adjoining sewage plants, though a pleasant public open space parallels the canal north of windlass-operated (but handcuff-locked) lift-bridge No.1. Close by a plaque celebrates Mary Moffat, who was born at Plantation Farm, Dukinfield, a small holding set in a strange no man's land between the canal and the river. An African missionary, she was said to have been an

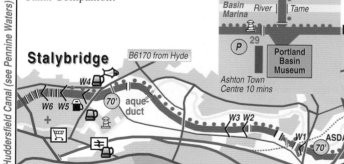

Huddersfield Canal (see Pennine Waters)

Stalybridge

W4
W6 W5
70'
aqueduct
W3 W2
W1
ASDA
70'
B6170 from Hyde

PORTLAND BASIN

Portland Basin Marina
River | Tame
P 29
Portland Basin Museum
Ashton Town Centre 10 mins

Dukin-field

8
sewage works
3
70'
2
sewage works

Cheshire Ring

Audenshaw

Audenshaw Reservoirs
Fairfield
70'
21 20 19 18
Jam Factory

1
27
26
24
25

Guide Bridge

GUIDE BRIDGE
mills

28
26
29
Portland Basin

Ashton-under-Lyne

A635   M'CHESTER

N

***Figures refer to Cheshire Ring route.**

inspiration to her son-in-law, one David Livingstone.

The Ashton Canal

PORTLAND BASIN is overlooked by a lofty mill chimney with what appears to be a crown on its head. Curiously, it belongs to a 'collector' of abandoned chimneys, a hobby which makes canal boating seem almost respectably sane. West of here, the Ashton makes its way to and from Manchester through a landscape of mills and abandoned (and now largely disappeared) collieries.

At GUIDE BRIDGE it encounters a cat's cradle of railway lines. In the mid Fifties this was briefly the point where steam propulsion gave way to electricity for the Trans-Pennine journey through Woodhead Tunnel to Sheffield; Britain's first, much vaunted, electrified main line. Twenty-five years later the route had closed, largely because the voltage first used didn't match that of later schemes. Integrated transport is a side of the British character well hidden.

A side bridge remains intact over the entrance to the site of Princess Dock, an early rail/canal transhipment point. The distinctive smell of marmalade issues from Robertson's large - and well kept - works at Bridge 18, as does also the constant rattle of jars. New bridges carrying Manchester's M60 orbital motorway and associated link roads are recent additions to the Ashton Canal scene hereabouts.

Rose Hill 'Tunnel'

Romiley — Map 8

Suburban settlement with bustling main street and useful shops best reached from Bridge 14. There's a highly recommended fish & chip shop/restaurant called WILSONS (Tel: 0161 494 8391) east of the railway station on Compstall Road. Somerfield supermarket, pharmacy and banks as well. Local trains provide connections with Marple, Hyde etc to the advantage of towpath walkers. Tel: 08457 484950.

Ashton-under-Lyne — Map 9

Old textile and mining town notable in that it once had an extensive trolleybus system. Once all these satellites in Manchester's solar system must have seemed more self sufficiently autonomous, now their economies rely on those too poor or immobile to visit 'big brother' to go about their business. Yet an old pride lingers in the weather-beaten faces of the more elderly locals and, met half way, their town more than repays a visit from passing canallers. Failing that, you could try a faith-healing session in the Town Hall, Mondays 11am to 3pm. Incidentally, this was the birthplace, in 1892, of the travel writer H.V. Morton.

The Market Hall is breathtaking, and it is quite possible to lose your womenfolk in it for hours on end while you attend to more serious matters, like a meat pie from S. Williams & Sons.

WENDY'S MEMORY LANE - Stamford Street. Characterful tea room knee-deep in memorabilia. Tel: 0161 330 2771.

TOURIST INFORMATION - Market Street. Tel: 0161 343 4343.

PORTLAND BASIN INDUSTRIAL MUSEUM (Tel: 0161 343 1978, openTue-Sun 10am-5pm, admission free) provides a detailed insight into the area's industrial past. It's housed in a canalside warehouse built by the Ashton Canal Company in 1834. Though partially destroyed by fire in 1972, it continues to feature a 24ft diameter waterwheel used to power the internal hoists and associated machinery.

TRAINS - frequent services to/from Manchester Victoria, Stalybridge and Huddersfield. Tel: 08457 484950.
BUSES - Tel: 0161 228 7811. Useful links throughout the Tame Valley.

*T*HE ASHTON was at its busiest in the middle of the 19th century when annual tonnages carried were in the giddy region of half a million. A hundred years later this had declined to a few thousand. In 1957 only seventeen tons are recorded as having been carried and by the following year all trade had ceased. In 1961 vandals set fire to Lock 11, virtually destroying it. Thereafter, until the glorious re-opening of 1974, the canal was effectively useless as a through route.

This is the part of the Cheshire Ring which boaters have had nightmares about. Bedevilled by hooliganism since its re-opening in 1974, there have been times when the perceived threat has been so pronounced that boats have been police-escorted through the flight. But the east side of Manchester is slowly being gentrified, and each time we come to renew our acquaintance with the purlieus of Ancoats, Clayton and Fairfield, they seem less intimidating than previously. Not that the natives have yet simmered down sufficiently to allow British Waterways to remove the

locks which protect the paddle gear from misuse - seventy-two sets in total (plus a pair of similarly restricted swing-bridges) - a more disconcerting aspect of the flight than any threat of vandalism, latent or otherwise.

So much for the Ashton's hazards; what of its ambience and atmosphere? Some of you will regard this as equally depressing, others will positively revel in its historic nuances, lost branches and industrial backdrop. Going down, Manchester is spread emphatically below you; going up, the grey, green tops of Saddleworth Moor beckon enticingly, and you are apt to find yourself humming that old hymn about 'Hills of the North Rejoicing'. Towpath travellers have time to take this all in. Boaters are likely to be too involved with the onerous task of unlocking, then re-locking all that paddle gear to enjoy much of the view.

The Ashton Canal's eighteen locks comprise the following

> **Don't forget you need special handcuff keys to unlock the locked paddle gear on all the locks and swingbridges between Ancoats and Fairfield.**

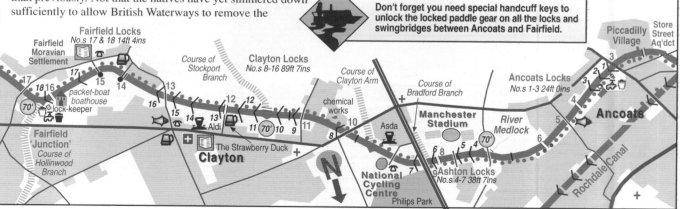

flights: Fairfield (2); Clayton (9); Ashton (formerly known as Beswick) (4) and Ancoats (3). From FAIRFIELD JUNCTION a branch canal was built to Hollinwood on the outskirts of Oldham. Its terminus lay less than a mile from the Rochdale Canal, but though a link was mooted, it never materialised. Collieries provided the Hollinwood Branch with most of its trade, but a recreational element also flourished at 'Crime Lake' a Tixall-like widening which attracted boathouses, tea rooms and fairground booths to its banks.

The short pound between formerly duplicated locks 17 and 18 is spanned by a stone footbridge (known locally as the camel's hump) with a strong family resemblance to the roving bridge at Portland Basin. Also of interest is a boathouse which housed a packet boat prior to the coming of the railways. Near at hand is Fairfield Moravian Settlement, a secluded and strangely unworldly estate of Georgian town housing built about cobbled avenues lit by cast iron lamps. The Moravians are a Protestant sect founded in Europe during the 15th century.

CLAYTON LOCKS lie amidst a plethora of chemical factories. The "Strawberry Duck", by Lock 13 (Tel: 0161 223 4415) provides food, locally brewed Holts beer and a warm welcome on the opposite bank. Nearby, Stockport 'Junction' marks the egress point of a five mile branch which never actually reached Stockport, petering out instead by the flour-caked, redbrick mills of South Reddish. In common with the Hollinwood Branch, its trade ceased in the early Thirties, though official abandonment, in both cases, didn't occur until 1961. Similarly, there was a degree of leisure use, rowing boats being available for hire from the Pomona Inn at Gorton.

You'll be beginning to appreciate that each flight has a flavour of its own. Above Lock 6 at BESWICK an arm extended into the precincts of Bradford Colliery whilst, opposite, stood an electricity generating station. These seem like ghosts now that the National Cycling Centre and City of Manchester Stadium - collectively known as SportCity - have transformed the surroundings. The boatmen of the 19th century would have been astonished by such developments. Manchester City Football Club now occupy the stadium which was originally constructed for the

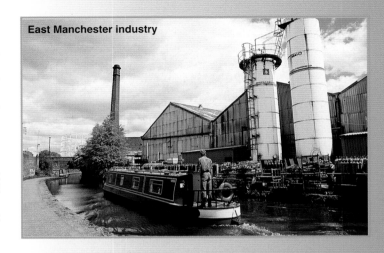

East Manchester industry

Commonwealth Games - Tours are available, telephone 0870 062 1894.

ANCOATS LOCKS - in recent years overlooked by a decaying zone of abandoned textile mills - lie at the centre of a redevelopment zone. Urban Splash are behind the scheme, and they are employing the architect Will Alsop whose keynote building will be known as 'Chips', three stories of apartments angled against each other like fat chips on a plate. A new canal arm will reflect this avant-garde architecture in all its glory, a far cry from the past when this area was littered with canal arms of an altogether different ambience. Long gone, for example, the manure wharf, a euphemism for the transhipment point of raw sewage and Corporation horse droppings onto narrowboats for carriage out into the city's rural hinterland for use as fertilizer. Another feature to be incorporated, in what will become known as New Islington, will be houses on stilts with space to moor a boat beneath, a laudable approach to canalside redevelopment, far more exciting than the rather tepid embrace of the PICCADILLY VILLAGE.

QUARTER of a century ago, when we published the first edition of the *Cheshire Ring Canal Companion*, received wisdom discouraged tarrying in Manchester. You moored overnight in Romiley or Sale, cast furtively off at dawn, and did a twelve hour stint at the tiller. Manchester was so synonymous with decay and vandalism that it was regarded by the majority of canal travellers as a necessary evil, a temporary aberration in the otherwise predominantly scenic character of the Cheshire Ring. Times have changed! Revitalisation and refurbishment - both on the canals and throughout much of the adjoining urban environment - have transformed the canal journey through Manchester into (in our opinion at any rate) one of the highlights of the Cheshire Ring. Personally, we find these canals so attractive and intriguing now that we would gladly moor up for a week here, content to use the boat as a base for exploring the many fascinating aspects of this vibrant city.

The Canals of Piccadilly

Piccadilly (nee Dale Street) Basin is a possible point to moor - night or day - between the Ashton and Rochdale flights, though correspondents suggest that it is best to do so along the south wall adjoining Ducie Street. Once this part of Manchester had a large number of canal wharves and warehouses. Now, after years of being ignored, it is becoming a fashionable part of the city to live in. The basin adjoins the junction of the Ashton and Rochdale canals a stone's throw from Piccadilly station on the south-eastern edge of the city centre. Re-opening of the Rochdale Canal eastward has brought new life to the basin and eradicated much of the seedier aspect it once endured. There are a few tangible remains of the Rochdale's prouder past: a crenellated entry arch of Dale Street itself; the canal company's offices; and a substantial warehouse still revealing its former water arches.

The Rochdale Nine

Entrance to this wide beam flight of locks is restricted to between the hours of 8 and 6 - for further information contact British Waterways at their Warrington office on 01925 847700. Immediately below the top lock (No.84 in the sequence which starts at Sowerby Bridge) the canal plunges into subterranean gloom and the boater has to steer gingerly between concrete columns supporting the eighteen storey Rodwell Tower office block. This twilight zone has enjoyed a seedy reputation down the years. Disconcerting as this can be, it bears remembering that there have been no reported incidents of canal users ever being assaulted.

The second lock (No.85) does a passable impression of what the Styx would have looked like if Brindley had ever been called in to make it navigable. But daylight returns beyond Piccadilly and you emerge to the rumbling of trams over Aytoun Street. The Rochdale Nine are endlessly entertaining, providing the canal traveller with an offbeat, quirky and provocative aspect of the city, an adventurous alternative to the more obvious tourist and visitor based thoroughfares. Canal Street lies at the heart of Manchester's now famous Gay Village, venue of the annual provocatively, yet amusingly titled 'It's Queer Up North' festival. By Lock 87 a Beacon of Hope sculpture is dedicated to all affected by HIV and AIDS. In the neighbouring little plot of green the sculptured figure of a man on a park bench holding an apple in his palm commemorates Alan Turing, codebreaker at Bletchley Park during World War Two, and father of computer science at Manchester University in the early Fifties. Turing ate an apple laced with cyanide in 1954 because his homosexuality had been exposed and he had become a victim of prejudice.

Over Princess Street double-decker buses create a kaleidoscope of colour, enlivening the muted tones of massive textile warehouses refurbished as flats, hotels and restaurants. Turn right into Whitworth Street and you'll be confronted by the astonishing Edwardian Baroque of India House. Built in 1906, it featured in Adolphe Valette's painting of the same name. Bloom Street Power Station overlooks the pound between locks 87 and 88. It was built in 1902, primarily to provide power for Manchester's tramways, but surplus steam was harnessed to provide heating for shops and offices in the vicinity, it was even used to raise the curtain at the Palace Theatre. Manchester's own Oxford Street spans the

continued an page 28

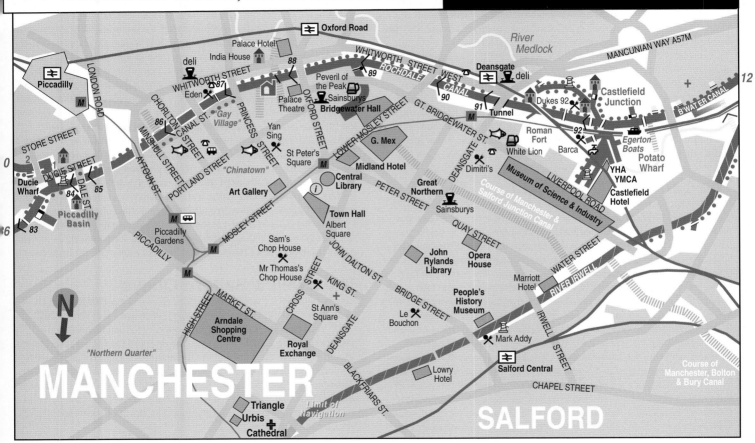

This map to scale: 3.5 inches to a mile.

continued from page 26

canal, the canalscape here being dominated by the terracotta tower of Sir Alfred Waterhouse's Refuge Assurance building, now the Palace Hotel. Then comes Lock 89 and the former junction with the Manchester & Salford Junction Canal, a section of which was rewatered to connect with the Halle Orchestra's Bridgewater Hall.

Between Locks 90 and 91 a split level boardwalk development of clubs and bars known as "Deansgate Locks" occupies former railway arches. Towards the foot of the flight the canal passes through a short tunnel under Deansgate and is then crossed by a handsome castellated railway bridge. The bottom chamber is known as Duke's Lock because it was actually built by the Bridgewater company. Later it was renumbered in the Rochdale sequence, the 92nd lock on the canal's epic Trans-Pennine journey from Sowerby Bridge.

The Canals of Castlefield

Doyen of the Canal Age, the Bridgewater arrived at Castlefield in 1765: George III was on the throne and America was still a British colony. Forty years were to pass before the Rochdale Canal came to join the Bridgewater. Everyone knows that the latter was dug to carry the Duke of Bridgewater's coals from his mines at Worsley (Map 24) to the market place of Manchester, but the canal soon developed as a general carrier and numerous warehouses sprang into being at Castlefield for the storage of multifarious cargoes. Several remain intact. Dominating the junction, the Merchants Warehouse has been refurbished, as has the vast Middle Warehouse overlooking the arm leading to the River Medlock. At the end of this arm, at a point where the original canal tunnelled beneath the sandstone outcrop, stands the Grocers Warehouse. Dating from the 18th century, the building originally consisted of five floors with a central arch over the canal. Later a second arch was added. An ingenious system of sluices fed a water wheel which drove the warehouse's lifting machinery. Two floors topped by a viewing promenade have been reconstructed, whilst the former bays are fronted by a pair of not entirely appropriate nor aesthetically pleasing metal lift bridges.

But it would be churlish to be pedantically critical of Castlefield. Some observers have cited the relatively new footbridge which spans the junction as being out of keeping with the largely 19th century environment surrounding it, but we feel it complements the adjoining railway structures without ingratiatingly replicating them. It is wider at its centre so as to provide space for pedestrians to pause to take in the view, and was inspired by Calatrava's Ripoll Bridge in Gerona. The railway viaducts are of enormous aesthetic appeal. See how the original masonry arches have been parodied in cast iron. One set of tracks carries conventional trains, the other, higher level, forms the Metrolink tramway approach to G. Mex, the former Central Station reborn as an exhibition and sports hall.

A series of arms extend beneath these railway arches towards Liverpool Road and the Museum of Science & Industry. Overlooked by the Castlefield Hotel, they provide probably the best casual moorings in Manchester, right at the heart of things. This area was known as POTATO WHARF, a name reflecting the use of these arms as an unloading point for market garden produce brought in by boat from the farmlands of Cheshire and Staffordshire. On the opposite side of the Bridgewater Canal stood SLATE WHARF, now revived as a name for a housing complex complete with its own basin reached beneath a towpath lift bridge.

The Irwell & Salford Quays

Access to the River Irwell and Salford Quays is via POMONA LOCK located on Map 12; Hulme Lock - its predecessor - was abandoned in 1992. Your passage will have to be booked in advance through the Manchester Ship Canal Company - see overleaf for further information. Should you have the time and the inclination, though, we can heartily recommend a detour onto the Irwell, navigable upstream as far as the Cathedral, and downstream to Salford Quays. And although this amounts to little more than two miles of highly urbanised river navigation, it makes for a fascinating journey, offering a unique aspect of the twin cities of Manchester and Salford.

Canal Street 1

Canal Street 2

30

The pace of change in Manchester is so furious that each new edition of this guide feels like a fresh introduction to a relative stranger. Manchester seems like a city on an ever upward trajectory, reinventing itself post-industrially with a fervour that one can only admire, even if it borders on the obsessive. The sadness, from the canaller's viewpoint, is that Manchester's act of embrace with its waterways appears not to be returned with equal affection. Unlike Birmingham, say, canalside redevelopments here appear less well integrated; more a matter of passive reflection than direct involvement. The best part of fifteen years have passed since Castlefield's canals were refurbished, though boat movements remain at such a relatively low level that it sometimes feels like a party which disappointingly few invitees have bothered to attend.

Architecturally, however, Manchester remains inherently one of the most handsome cities in the industrial world, and we would urge you to moor and explore; nothing's very far away, the city centre being astonishingly compact and approachable. 'Musts' include the three squares: Albert with Waterhouse's imposing Town Hall; St Ann's, an oasis of peace in the city centre; and St Peter's, dominated by the circular Central Library and flamboyant terracotta of the Midland Hotel, meeting place (4th May, 1904) of a certain Mr Rolls with a certain Mr Royce. More esoterically, try venturing into the rag trade zone east of Piccadilly and thence to High Street where the old Wholesale Fish Market boasts astonishing friezes. Or wander your way down to the banks of the Irwell where, in the shadow of the modest cathedral lies Chethams Music School, Victoria Station and the solidly confident Co-operative buildings. These are the parts of Manchester reassuringly Northern in character. The smoke palls may have been blown away by the winds of change, but there are moments when it is still possible to feel that you've walked on to a canvas by Adolphe Valette or his pupil L. S. Lowry.

DUKES 92 - canalside by Lock 92, Castlefield Junction. Elegant, but egalitarian establishment offering a bewildering choice of cheeses and pates.Tel: 0161 839 8646.

MARK ADDY - Stanley Street, Salford. Tel: 0161 832 4080. Sister establishment to Dukes 92, the Mark Addy derives its name from a local man who rescued over fifty people from drowning in the river, being the only civilian ever to be awarded the Victoria Cross. The pub was opened in the 1980s on the site of a former packet boat landing stage and attracts a wide variety of custom.

EDEN - Canal Street. Canalside and candle-lit in the heart of the Gay Village; try the Starigrad Lamb. Tel: 0161 237 9852.

WHITE LION - Liverpool Road. Tel: 0161 832 7373. CAMRA recommended pub across the road from the Museum of Science & Industry.

DIMITRI'S - Campfield Arcade, Castlefield. Lively and atmospheric Greek tapas bar and taverna. Tel: 0161 839 3319.

PEVERIL OF THE PEAK - Gt Bridgewater Street (near Lock 89). Famous green-tiled pub. Tel: 0161 236 6364.

JOLLY ANGLER - Ducie Street. Friendly basic boozer featuring locally brewed Hydes. Tel: 0161 236 5307.

YANG SING - Princess Street. Renowned Chinese. Tel: 0161 236 2200.

LE BOUCHON - Bridge Street. Tel: 0161 832 9393. French restaurant.

MR THOMAS'S CHOP HOUSE - Cross Street. A Manchester Institution. Tel: 0161 832 2245.

The principal shopping area lies to the north of the Rochdale Canal, and that, Ladies, is below the line of the canal on Map 11. There are excellent delis adjacent to locks 87 and 91, and a handy Sainsbury's Express on Oxford Street.

TOURIST INFORMATION - St Peter's Square. Tel: 0161 234 3157.

MUSEUM OF SCIENCE & INDUSTRY - Liverpool Road. Open daily 10am to 5pm. Tel: 0161 832 1830. First class celebration of Manchester's industrial prowess and scientific endeavour. Free admission.

CITY ART GALLERY - Mosley Street. Tel: 0161 234 1456. Access is free to this inspiring and recently much refurbished gallery.

URBIS - Cathedral Gardens. Tel: 0161 907 9099. A new celebration of metropolitan life.

PEOPLE'S HISTORY MUSEUM - Bridge Street. Open Tue-Sun. Admission free on Fridays. Tel: 0161 839 6061. A look at the lives of ordinary people in Britain over the last two hundred years.

IMPERIAL WAR MUSEUM - Trafford Wharf Road. Tel: 0161 877 9240. 'How people's lives are shaped by war.'

THE LOWRY - Salford Quays. An inspiring mix of galleries, theatres, shops and restaurants - what would the curmudgeonly old bachelor of Mottram have made of it? Easiest access from Castlefield by Metrolink from G-Mex stop. Tel: 0161 876 2000.

MANCHESTER UNITED MUSEUM & TOUR - Tel: 0161 868 8631. Visitor moorings available right alongside 'The Reds' huge stadium.

LOCAL BUS, RAIL & TRAM - Tel: 0161 228 7811.

INTERCITY TRAINS - Tel: 08457 484950.

UNLIKE the canals' eastern entrance and exit to and from the centre of Manchester, the Bridgewater is entirely without locks, and so the boater has more time to savour the never less than interesting environment they are passing through. WATERS MEETING is a

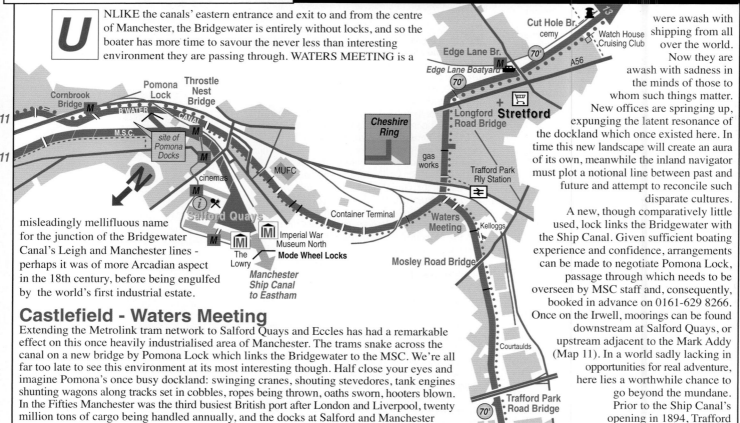

were awash with shipping from all over the world. Now they are awash with sadness in the minds of those to whom such things matter. New offices are springing up, expunging the latent resonance of the dockland which once existed here. In time this new landscape will create an aura of its own, meanwhile the inland navigator must plot a notional line between past and future and attempt to reconcile such disparate cultures.

A new, though comparatively little used, lock links the Bridgewater with the Ship Canal. Given sufficient boating experience and confidence, arrangements can be made to negotiate Pomona Lock, passage through which needs to be overseen by MSC staff and, consequently, booked in advance on 0161-629 8266. Once on the Irwell, moorings can be found downstream at Salford Quays, or upstream adjacent to the Mark Addy (Map 11). In a world sadly lacking in opportunities for real adventure, here lies a worthwhile chance to go beyond the mundane.

Prior to the Ship Canal's opening in 1894, Trafford

misleadingly mellifluous name for the junction of the Bridgewater Canal's Leigh and Manchester lines - perhaps it was of more Arcadian aspect in the 18th century, before being engulfed by the world's first industrial estate.

Castlefield - Waters Meeting

Extending the Metrolink tram network to Salford Quays and Eccles has had a remarkable effect on this once heavily industrialised area of Manchester. The trams snake across the canal on a new bridge by Pomona Lock which links the Bridgewater to the MSC. We're all far too late to see this environment at its most interesting though. Half close your eyes and imagine Pomona's once busy dockland: swinging cranes, shouting stevedores, tank engines shunting wagons along tracks set in cobbles, ropes being thrown, oaths sworn, hooters blown. In the Fifties Manchester was the third busiest British port after London and Liverpool, twenty million tons of cargo being handled annually, and the docks at Salford and Manchester

24

Park was the country seat of the De Trafford family who had held sway here since the 11th century. In 1896 they were made an offer they obviously found hard to refuse, for two years later work started on the development of the world's first industrial estate which, at its zenith during the Second World War, included two hundred firms employing over seventy thousand people. Trafford Park Village was developed to house incoming workers. It was modelled on the American gridiron pattern, with streets and avenues given numbers rather than names.

Manchester United's iconic Old Trafford stadium overlooks the Bridgewater Canal by Warwick Road Bridge. It must be a moving experience to pass here when a game is taking place, with sixty plus thousand souls roaring on their team. On the towpath side mooring pins recall where barges, travelling down from collieries in the vicinity of Worsley, Leigh and Wigan, delivered coal to Trafford Park power station until 1972. The canal traffic's decline mirrored the football team's. United were at their post-war nadir, being relegated, at the end of the 73/74 season to the wilderness of Division Two. Such embarrassments seem far fetched now. Astute financial husbandry has built a footballing dynasty of immense wealth and security. Yet, as we went to press, the club had fallen into the hands of an American financier called Glazer, and suddenly the future seemed less well-defined.

Juggernauts ply to and from the container terminal alongside the canal which seems to have enjoyed a new lease of life following the opening of the Channel Tunnel. Freight from the south of Spain can be unloaded here in the same time that it used to take to arrive from East Lancs! This is not to say that transport by canal has no further role to play in the twenty-first century. Non-time sensitive commodities could still effectively be carried by water if the right incentives were put in place. Successive governments continue to pay political lip service to the concept of canal carrying, but rarely does any real traffic materialise. The container depot occupies the site of Trafford Park motive power depot which was operated by the Cheshire Lines Committee. For many years it was home to a stud of J. G. Robinson's handsome 'Director' class 4-4-0 locomotives.

Waters Meeting - Stretford

Progressing in a westerly direction, industry begins to make way for the suburbs and vice versa. Longford Road Bridge marks the temporary terminus of the Bridgewater Canal from Worsley between 1761 and 1765, before Castlefield was reached. On the outside bend, south of the bridge, stood Rathbone's, a notable drydock and boatbuilding yard where work still goes on, albeit on a much reduced scale. Watch House Cruising Club occupy a former length-man's cottage overlooking a series of arches which carry the canal over the Mersey Valley. Boat clubs are a feature of the Bridgewater Canal these days, but it wasn't until 1952 that pleasure cruising was permitted at all. In the Fifties the Watch House was base for a horse-drawn hotel boat operation which plied canals all over the country. When the Bridgewater Canal opened it stimulated the development of its hinterland for market gardening. It seems difficult to believe now that Stretford was once a centre for pig rearing!

Waters Meeting - Barton upon Irwell

North-west of Waters Meeting the Bridgewater Canal is immediately submerged in the precincts of Trafford Park industrial estate which keeps it company all the way to Barton, though, it has to be said, the canal seems to eschew dialogue with the businesses on its banks, being brutally separated from them by tall, barbed wire-topped fences. In the majority of cases the canal didn't play much part in the development of these industries, but two notable exceptions were the carriage of chemicals by Cowburn & Cowpar narrowboats to and from Courtaulds, and the use of barges to bring grain from Salford Docks to Kelloggs who built a works here just prior to the Second World War as part of an initially ill-timed drive to enter the European health food market. The use of barges continued until 1974. Merchant ships carrying up to 10,000 tons of American grain would tranship their cargoes into a fleet of Bridgewater barges. A roving bridge carries the towpath over the arm into which the barges entered the works for unloading by suction into the high silos. Nowadays the grain for your breakfast cereals is transported by lorry from Seaforth Grain Terminal on the Mersey at Liverpool.

*T*HE Bridgewater Canal traverses the seemingly interminable suburbs of Sale and Altrincham, an urban sprawl broken only by the green corridor of the Mersey's flood plain. There are decent moorings by Sale Bridge and access to a wide range of facilities.

It is odd to reflect that none of these buildings were here when Brindley charted the Bridgewater cut across the flat peat mosses towards the Runcorn Gap in the middle of the 18th century. Indeed, this area remained predominantly agricultural (its fecundity enhanced by daily cargoes of 'night soil' from inner Manchester) until construction of the Manchester, South Junction & Altrincham Railway brought an explosion of house building in its wake from the 1840s onwards. Before they actually built the railway there were proposals to convert the canal into one. Thankfully, nothing came of that, but the trains did bring an end to the passenger packet boat services hitherto operated.

With the railway came commuters. In 1850 Sale was just a rifle range for army volunteers to practice on, whilst Altrincham was a modest market town of less than four thousand souls. Fifty years later they had amassed a combined population of 100,000. The train service was intensive and electrified as early as 1931. Nowadays it is operated as part of Manchester's 'Metrolink' light railway, a rapid transit system which restored trams to the city's streets for the first time since 1949.

Just north of the M60 an aqueduct carries the canal over the River Mersey. Even after the development of Sale, building stopped short of the flood plain, leaving a cummerbund of emerald silk about the burgeoning waistline of Greater Manchester. Sale Water Park has been created out of gravel extraction cavities associated with the construction of the motorway and is popular with windsurfers, water skiers and small boat sailors. Another form of leisure is evident at Manchester University's sports ground and rowing club premises near White's Bridge. Sale is, in fact, something of a centre of sporting excellence in this region, boasting both a well respected rugby union team, the Sale Harriers athletic club, and Trafford Rowing Club whose crews have been put through their paces on the Bridgewater Canal since the Nineteen Fifties.

At Broadheath look out for the Linotype Works of 1897; the majestic old cotton warehouse with its arched loading bay for boats; the horse-steps provided for the rescue of boat horses who had slipped into the canal; and the hand operated cranes which are such a feature of Bridgewater bridges - they're used for lifting stop planks into place so that the canal can be drained for maintenance or in an emergency.

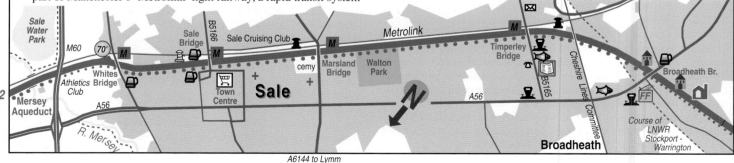

O UTSKIRTS have their own remoteness; a quality exaggerated by the sense of contrast between what is urban and what is rural. Greater Manchester's sprawl hasn't quite extended to its boundary with Cheshire. Oldfield Brow marks the last (or first in the case of eastbound travellers) of the conurbation. Dunham Town sits as pretty as a picture in the fragility of no man's land. From hereabouts to Romiley - the first semblance of countryside on the far side of Manchester - it is ten hours cruising. Gone, though, are the days when we would have exhorted you to avoid mooring overnight in the city.

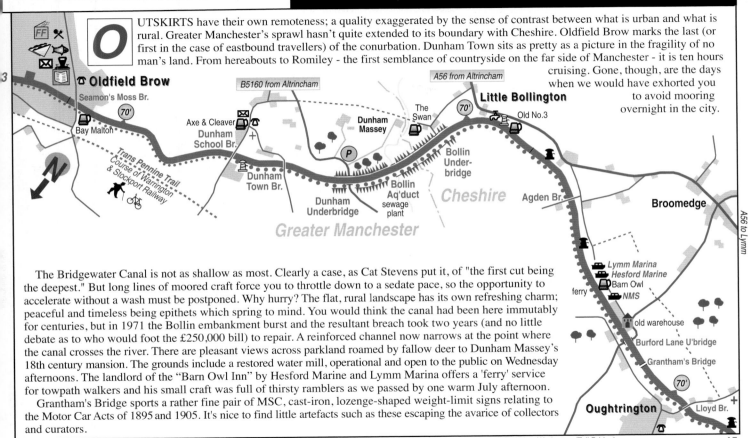

The Bridgewater Canal is not as shallow as most. Clearly a case, as Cat Stevens put it, of "the first cut being the deepest." But long lines of moored craft force you to throttle down to a sedate pace, so the opportunity to accelerate without a wash must be postponed. Why hurry? The flat, rural landscape has its own refreshing charm; peaceful and timeless being epithets which spring to mind. You would think the canal had been here immutably for centuries, but in 1971 the Bollin embankment burst and the resultant breach took two years (and no little debate as to who would foot the £250,000 bill) to repair. A reinforced channel now narrows at the point where the canal crosses the river. There are pleasant views across parkland roamed by fallow deer to Dunham Massey's 18th century mansion. The grounds include a restored water mill, operational and open to the public on Wednesday afternoons. The landlord of the "Barn Owl Inn" by Hesford Marine and Lymm Marina offers a 'ferry' service for towpath walkers and his small craft was full of thirsty ramblers as we passed by one warm July afternoon.

Grantham's Bridge sports a rather fine pair of MSC, cast-iron, lozenge-shaped weight-limit signs relating to the Motor Car Acts of 1895 and 1905. It's nice to find little artefacts such as these escaping the avarice of collectors and curators.

Oldfield Brow
Map 14

Outer suburb of Altrincham with handy facilities for canallers including a shop (with cash machine), post office, cafe (Tel: 0161 929 4174), sandwich bar (Tel: 0161 929 8100), Tandoori (Tel: 0161 924 0161) and fish & chips (Tel: 0161 941 1127). Canalside, stands the BAY MALTON (Tel: 0161 928 0655) pub named after a racehorse.

Dunham
Map 14

Quaint estate village with a nice country pub called the AXE & CLEAVER (Tel: 0161 928 3391) and a tiny post office store.

(i) DUNHAM MASSEY HALL & PARK - house open late Mar-end Sept, Sat-Wed, 12-5pm, weekends only during Oct. Garden open Mar-Oct, daily 11-5.30pm. Shop and restaurant open daily throughout the year (except Christmas). Parkland open daily throughout the year. Sawmill usually in operation on Weds & Sats Apr-Oct. Tel: 0161 941 1025. Admission charge. Dunham Massey Hall was bequeathed to the National Trust by the 10th Earl of Stamford in 1976. It features one of Britain's most sumptuous Edwardian interiors. Over thirty rooms are open to the public housing an admirable collection of furniture, paintings and Huguenot silver. Fallow deer roam in the 250 acres of delightful parkland.

Lymm
Map 15

One of the most appealing 'ports of call' on the 'Cheshire Ring', and its facilities could not be handier. Take a walk up The Dingle to The Dam, a man-made lake with nature trails and picnic tables. Lymm also provides access to the Trans Pennine Trail which has hereabouts adopted the old Warrington-Stockport railway line which runs parallel to the canal between Oldfield Brow and Latchford, thereby offering the potential of several circular walks when combined with the towpath.

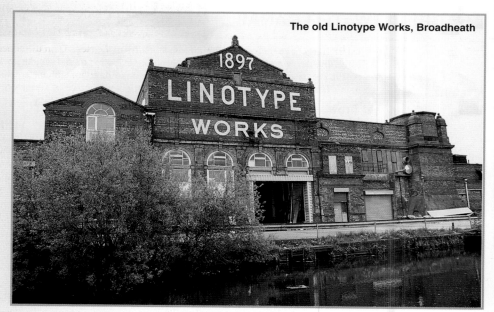

The old Linotype Works, Broadheath

TRATTORIA BACI - The Cross. Tel: 01925 756067. Italian restaurant.
LYMM BISTRO - Eagle Brow. Tel: 01925 754852.
SEXTONS - Eagle Brow. Tel: 01925 753669. Cafe (with internet facilities) serving fresh baking. Fine shop also - see below.
There are several pubs within easy reach of the canal with opportunities for connoisseurs to sample Manchester brewed beers by Hydes and Lees. Also near at hand are take-aways, an Indian restaurant and fish & chips.

Conscious of its charm, boutique and antique outlets have infiltrated the more traditional retailers. There's a Somerfield supermarket, a butcher, SEXTONS excellent bakery (which does take-away/ready cooked meals), pharmacy and wine merchants plus several banks. There's a nice little market every Thursday.

BUSES - services to/from Warrington and Altrincham. Tel: 0870 6082608.

Grappenhall
Map 15

A cobbled lane leads to the 16th century church and village stocks. A neat row of colonial-looking cottages separates two pleasant pubs: the RAMS HEAD and the PARR ARMS.

UNOSTENTATIOUSLY true to its 83ft contour, the Bridgewater Canal slips through the dainty little town of Lymm and glides past the villages of Thelwall and Grappenhall. And the boater has nothing more arduous to do, than swing the tiller from time to time, and watch the herons flap slowly away from the water's edge in an arc when their nerve breaks.

In canal terms, this twenty-five mile pound constitutes what the French would call the *longueurs* of the Cheshire Ring. So one welcomes the charm of Lymm and is grateful for an excuse to leave the canal behind and renew one's relationship with dry land. The inconspicuous Whitbarrow Aqueduct carries the canal over a brook which cleaves a dramatic gorge through a sandstone outcrop on its way down to the Mersey. The gorge has been turned into an attractive park, but once there was a mill here, the sluice and water wheel of which remain to tickle your historic fancy. Lymm was an early victim of transport engineering. Brindley surveyed a route which sliced the old town square in half, so that even today houses overhang Lymm Bridge like interrupted conversations.

An entertaining walk is there for the taking at Thelwall. Go down the steps from the aqueduct and pass beneath the old railway - they used to win prizes for their flower displays at Thelwall station before it closed in 1956 - cross the A56 and proceed down Bell Lane, bearing left by the village cross. On reaching the 'Pickering's Arms' pub (note the inscription commemorating the foundation of a settlement here - 'city' being something of an exaggeration - in 923 by the son of King Alfred the cake burner) turn right down Ferry Lane. Regulars will know of the enchantment ferries hold for us, and the Thelwall Ferry (operating hours 7-9am ex Sun, 12-2pm and 4-7pm) has always been one of our Cheshire ring treats. The ferryman will 'scull' you over to the far bank of the Manchester Ship Canal in his open boat, licensed to carry no more than nine passengers at a time. Having gained the far bank, a short walk westwards will bring you to the giant Latchford Locks. The larger of the two chambers measures 600 x 65ft - just think how many narrowboats you could fit in that. You can complete the circle by returning via the Trans Pennine Trail, a 215 miles long multi-user right of way linking Southport on the West Coast with Hornsea on the East.

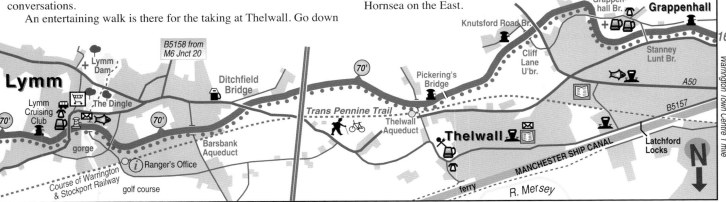

*I*N earlier, fire and brimstone editions of this Canal Companion we railed against the iniquities of Britain's transport policy (or dearth of it), urging you to stroll down from the Bridgewater Canal at Stockton Heath to see the Manchester Ship Canal, and thus marvel at the engineering advances made in a century and a quarter of canal building, at the same time regretting that so little commercial use be made of our inland waterways now. But we have mellowed with age, if not wisdom, and such sadnesses hardly ruffle our conscience these days. We have been to too many canal cargo funerals - last runs and last rites - to cry crocodile tears anymore. We're all holidaymakers now, glad that the Bridgewater's 18th century course steers clear of downtown Warrington, becoming no more urbanised than as manifested by the Victorian villas and bay-windowed semis of Stockton Heath.

Those with a penchant for the past are well served hereabouts: Lumbrook Underbridge has its date of build - 1770 - carved on its south facing stonework; the steps are still in place at Stockton Quay down which 18th century canal passengers would go to board the packet boats linking Runcorn with Manchester; whilst the premises of Thorn Marine (threatened with redevelopment) were originally occupied by the 'bank riders' of the packet boat horses. Indeed, the earnest student of inland waterway history is well served by Warrington, whose rivers, navigations and canals were all once busy trade routes, carrying commodities to and from the breweries, wire works, paper mills and soap factories which formed the staple industries of the town. During the 17th century the River Mersey was navigable as far upstream as Warrington. In 1736 the Mersey & Irwell Navigation constructed a series of weirs and locks to enable vessels to reach Manchester. Despite these improvements, navigation remained subject to tidal influence as far as Warrington, and craft were often stranded for lack of water. Opening of the Bridgewater Canal in 1773 captured much of the river trade. In retaliation, the Mersey & Irwell company built the Runcorn & Latchford Canal, by-passing the trickiest parts of the river. For the first half of the 19th century abundant trade kept both routes busy, but then the railways arrived, followed by the Ship Canal in 1894, and Warrington's canal network inevitably fell into a long, sad period of decline.

West of Stockton Heath, the canal journeys through charming countryside, negotiating a lush cutting ripe with rhododendrons at Higher Walton. Two railways scythe through Moore, that nearest the canal once being jointly owned by the Great Western Railway, a far flung outpost for a company more familiar with the haughty purlieus of Paddington. Look out for the log train, making its way from Arpley yard with Scottish timber for the Kronospan works at Chirk on the Llangollen Canal.

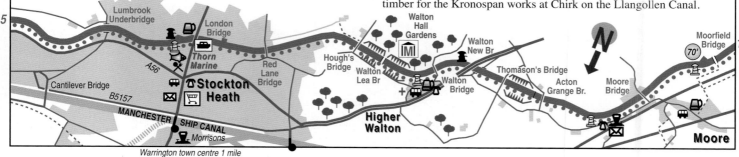

15

Lumbrook
Underbridge

London
Bridge

Thorn
Marine

A56

Cantilever Bridge

B5157

Stockton
Heath

MANCHESTER

SHIP CANAL

Morrisons

Warrington town centre 1 mile

Red
Lane
Bridge

Hough's
Bridge

Walton
Lea Br

Higher
Walton

Walton
Hall
Gardens

Walton
New Br

Walton
Bridge

Thomason's Bridge

Acton
Grange Br.

Moore
Bridge

Moorfield
Bridge

70'

17

Moore

Stockton Heath — Map 16

Bustling Warrington suburb useful for taking on provisions.

LONDON BRIDGE - canalside by London Bridge. Tel: 01925 267904. Smartly refurbished pub offering up to five guest ales and food 11am-9pm (noon start on Sundays). Canalside patio.

TOM AT 101 - London Road. Wine bar and restaurant just a couple of minutes walk down from the canal. Tel: 01925 212660.

PICCOLINO - London Road. Tel: 01925 211190. Stylish Italian restaurant, part of a growing chain.

PUCCINO'S - London Road. Tel: 01925 860677. Amusing cafe bar chain with restaurant evenings on Fridays and Saturdays.

Full range of facilities easily accessed from the canal. There's a handy SAINSBURY'S LOCAL on London Road, but much more intriguing is FOOD! (Tel: 01925 861200 www.foodforfood.co.uk) a delicatessen which sources items from around the world, Sicilian food being something of a speciality. Sandwiches are available at lunchtime to take out. Gateaux and patisserie. On the far side of the Ship Canal stands a large Morrisons supermarket. Frequent buses run into Warrington town centre which has an admirable indoor market, reputedly the largest in the North West.

Higher Walton — Map 16

Estate village built by the Greenall family who made their fortune brewing. Between the wars Sir Gilbert Greenall, Lord Daresbury, gained recognition as an expert breeder of horses and cattle. He died in 1938 and death duties led to the estate being sold. Warrington Council purchased the grandiose Elizabethan style hall and its grounds for an even then modest £19,000, but were forced to demolish sections of the house which were deemed beyond repair. Nevertheless, the gardens remain a popular destination for Warrington townsfolk, not least the rose garden, woodland walks, bandstand, bowling green, pitch & putt, heritage centre and children's zoo - Tel: 01925 601617. Close to the canal stands the WALTON ARMS - Tel: 01925 262659.

Moore — Map 16

Peaceful village despite its proximity to Runcorn. Home of the charmingly named Gentlemen of Moore Rugby Club. Good pub called the RED LION (Tel: 01925 740205), village stores and post office adjoining canal, and buses to/from Widnes and Runcorn. There is a nature reserve on the banks of the Manchester Ship Canal which runs to the north of the village.

Rhododendron cutting, Moore

Runcorn — Map 17A

Part of the Borough of Halton, which also embraces Widnes on the north bank of the Mersey, Runcorn is half old, half new; a former dockyard town with a Milton Keynes-like expansion grafted on. Aesthetically, some of the new town works, some of it doesn't, but the old town makes up for any such failures with the excitement of its setting overlooking the magnificent width of the river. A walk across Runcorn Bridge can be heartily recommended, perhaps coupled with a visit to CATALYST (Tel: 0151 420 1121) the science discovery centre at West Bank, Widnes on the far side.

THE BRINDLEY - canalside arts centre with bar and terrace cafe. Tel: 0151 907 8360. Numerous pubs and take-aways within easy reach of the canal.

Runcorn Shopping City on the outskirts, has all the chain stores but enough shops remain in the town centre to meet boaters' needs.

TOURIST INFORMATION - Church Street. Tel: 01928 576776.

NORTON PRIORY - Warrington Road. Canal access from Green's Bridge. Open daily from noon. Tel: 01928 569895. The museum celebrates three distinct layers of history which peel back to reveal: life in the original monastery dissolved by Henry VIII in 1536; the Tudor mansion which grew up in its place; and the Georgian country house of 1740 that succeeded it. On the opposite bank of the canal, Town Park boasts a delightful miniature railway in use on Sunday afternoons throughout the year - Tel: 01928 574396.

BUSES - an unusual feature of the town is its segregated 'busways', separate roads with access restricted to buses only, resulting in a fast 'interurban' network of services worth sampling for their own sake. Tel: 0870 608 2 608. TRAINS - station adjacent to canal terminus well served by trains to Liverpool, Crewe, Stafford, Milton Keynes and London Euston. Runcorn *East* station is on the Manchester, Warrington, Chester and North Wales route and is handily placed for Preston Brook. Tel: 08457 484950.

SCENIC sections of canal flank the old transhipment port of Preston Brook as the Bridgewater Canal gives way to the Trent & Mersey and vice versa. Between Moore and Preston Brook there are wide views over the Mersey Valley. Look out for Runcorn's massive suspension bridge, Fiddler's Ferry power station and, on the northern horizon, the Winter Hill radio mast up on Rivington Moor beyond Bolton. Closer to hand, the village of Daresbury has connections with Lewis Carroll. His father was curate here and characters from 'Alice in Wonderland' and 'Through the Looking Glass' are celebrated in the village church's stained glass windows. These days Daresbury is the home of a world renowned research laboratory which overlooks the canal. Futuristic as their research into the atom might be, however, they still rely on water from a two hundred years old canal for cooling purposes.

Preston Brook, location of the 2005 National Festival & Boat Show, was one of the busiest canal centres in the North-West, a port where cargoes were transhipped between wide beam Mersey 'flats' and narrowboats. A substantial number of warehouses were erected to cater for this activity, which continued right up until the end of the Second World War. Indeed, narrowboats continued to trade to and from Preston Brook as late as the 1970s, following which the majority of warehouses were regrettably demolished.

The actual demarcation between the Bridgewater and Trent & Mersey canals lies just inside the northern end of Preston Brook Tunnel. Not wide enough for boats to pass inside, the tunnel operates to a strict timetable, whereby southbound boats may enter the tunnel for ten minutes on the half hour; northbound on the hour for ten minutes. Make sure your watch is right! At the southern end of the tunnel the Trent & Mersey built a stop lock to protect their water supply. Nearby stands a drydock covered by a valanced canopy with a distinct sense of railway styling. Little wonder, the dock was built by the North Staffordshire Railway (for the maintenance of tunnel tugs) during their ownership of the canal between 1846 and 1923. Southwards, Trent & Mersey mileposts count down your progress towards Hardings Wood.

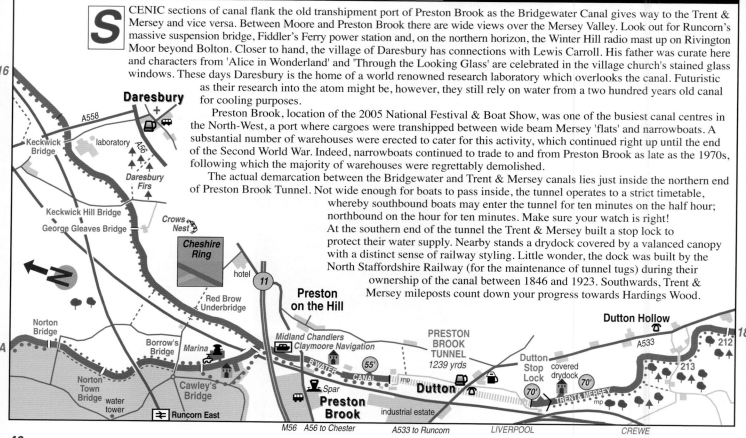

*I*N the past we have been taken to task for portraying the Runcorn Arm too austerely. Looking back, we don't think we were that harsh on it: "Runcorn's old town is an agreeable place to saunter around, especially if you have an affinity with the flotsam and jetsam of coastal ports." Less balanced observers have been far crueller to the arm's five lockless and predominantly urbanised miles, and hire boats are a relatively rare phenomenon, most boats on the move seemingly belonging to members of the Bridgewater Motor Boat Club which has premises in the old Sprinch boatbuilding yards at the western end of the canal.

But if boats are rare, towpath walking and cycling are activities enthusiastically embraced by the native population, as is angling. And there are rural interludes of a sort, notably in the vicinity of Greens Bridge where rhododendron shrubs fill the woods fringing the canal and moorings are provided for boaters wishing to visit Norton Priory. Here too lies the northern edge of Runcorn's Town Park which boasts an extensive miniature railway. West of Norton views open out over

the Manchester Ship Canal and the Mersey. This length used to be bordered by tanneries, producing leather for shoes and suitcases, harnesses and handbags.

Runcorn's non-league football ground has vanished beneath new housing since the previous edition of this guide materialised. Farmer or football club, it's all too tempting to take the money and run when property developers come knocking. Under the flight path for John Lennon, the canal approaches its foreshortened terminus, passing Co-operative Society premises, funeral parlours and pubs heavily shuttered out of hours. Stumps of old cranes hint that business was once brisk, but the arm meets its Waterloo, so to speak, at an ornately eponymous bridge which used to span the top chambers of the much mourned Runcorn Locks. From here two flights of ten locks each - the Old and New locks - led down to link with the Manchester Ship and Runcorn & Weston canals. Their controversial abandonment leaves present day boaters with no option other than to 'wind' and return to Preston Brook. Yes, explore the Runcorn Arm by all means, but go in with your eyes open ...

ONCE we would urge you to keep an eye out for shipping on the Weaver Navigation which runs parallel to the Trent & Mersey, albeit some distance below in the valley. Now, sadly - not to say incriminatingly - all the export output of the Northwich area's chemical and salt making industries is transported by road to the Mersey ports, leaving the Weaver bereft of commercial traffic for the first time in its history. What is it in our national character, what flaw in transportation theory, that leaves a perfectly adequate infrastructure like the Weaver, capable of supporting an environmentally harmonious mode of transport, devoid of traffic?

Inland shipping apart, this is an extremely beautiful length of the Trent & Mersey. Rolling farmland, interspersed with belts of deciduous woodland, characterise the canal's progress along a ledge above the Weaver's widening valley. Two tunnels add to the drama. Leaning back on the tiller, a glass of something mildly intoxicating in your hand, it's tempting to reflect that this is what canalling should always be like:

good scenery, good liquor and, "good grief, does that lunatic steering straight at you think he owns the cut!"

SALTERSFORD and BARNTON tunnels were amongst the earliest essays in the art of canal tunnel digging. They are far from straight. Neither are they wide enough for narrowboats to pass inside. Their lack of width also prevented widebeam barges from traversing the Trent & Mersey between Preston Brook and Middlewich as had originally been planned. They are short enough, however, not to cause undue traffic delays. Both bores are towpathless, but walkers and claustrophobics have the bonus of a charming walk, by way of the old horse paths, across the wooded tops. Separating the two tunnels is a an idyllic, leafy pool, which offers one of the Cheshire Ring's premier overnight mooring spots. You could linger here indefinitely, watching the boats emerge from the tunnels, and descending to the Weaver for a stroll along the well-maintained riverside path, whilst Barnton village offers just about all the products of civilisation one might ever need, recordings of Beethoven's late string quartets excepted.

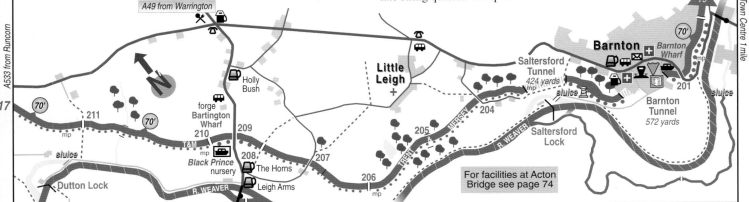

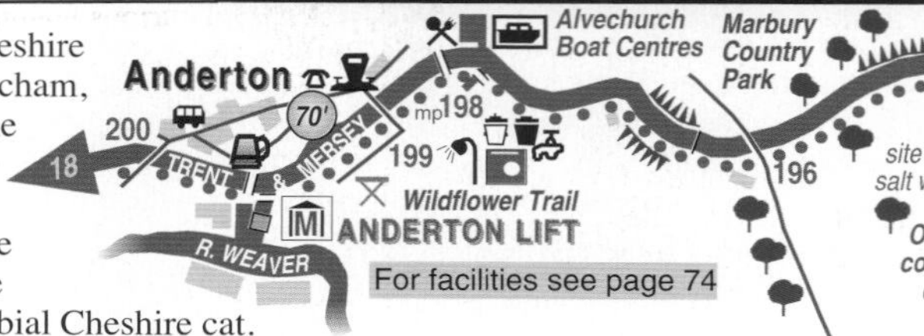

INDUSTRY returns to haunt the Cheshire Ring traveller at Anderton and Wincham, but the intrusion of factories into the green and pleasant landscape is thankfully short lived. Elsewhere on this section the canal threads its way through the peaceful farmlands of the Weaver and Dane valleys, as content with its lot as the proverbial Cheshire cat.

Of all the so called "Seven Wonders of the Waterways", ANDERTON LIFT is arguably the most ingenious, and it is marvellous to have it back in our midst, operating again as a link between the Trent & Mersey Canal and Weaver Navigation. If you're not planning to use it, at least moor up and watch it being put through its paces. Down on the banks of the Weaver a visitor centre supplies the facts and figures behind this astonishing contraption.

For our part, we describe The Lift in greater detail in the text accompanying Map 32. Meanwhile, the Trent & Mersey Canal continues on its unhurried way, negotiating a scarred landscape destabilised over the years by salt extraction. In 1958 a new length of canal had to be dug at Marston to by-pass a section bedevilled by subsidence.

LION SALT WORKS was the last in Britain to produce salt by the traditional method of evaporating brine in open pans. Sadly it was forced to close in 1986, by which time it was struggling to compete with modernised mass production techniques, but now it is slowly being restored as a working museum and visitor centre. At one time the works had its own small fleet of narrowboats plying between Marston and Anderton where the salt would be transhipped into larger vessels for export through the Mersey ports.

Between bridges 191 and 192 the canal is sandwiched between the stadia of two non-league football teams: Witton Albion, founded in 1887; and Northwich Victoria, founded in 1874. Two football clubs, with an average combined core spectatorship of less than two thousand, possessed of modern grounds separated solely by a canal - doesn't that illustrate the grandeur and folly of football perfectly!

The salt industry may have declined, but the production of chemicals continues to flourish hereabouts. The Brunner Mond works at Lostock dates from the late 19th century. Pipes spluttering with steam span the canal and lime waste is pumped across to the lagoons hidden by high embankments beyond the A530. The works, which has a handsome brick-built, Dutch-gabled office block, once had its own basin busy with canal craft.

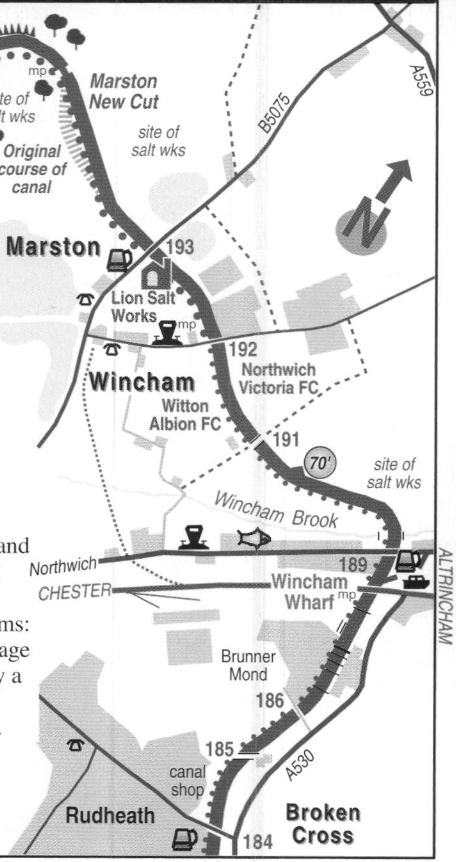

Anderton

Alvechurch Boat Centres

Marbury Country Park

Marston New Cut

site of salt wks

Original course of canal

Wildflower Trail

ANDERTON LIFT

R. WEAVER

For facilities see page 74

Marston

Lion Salt Works

Wincham

Witton Albion FC

Northwich Victoria FC

Wincham Brook

site of salt wks

Northwich

CHESTER

Wincham Wharf

Brunner Mond

canal shop

Rudheath

Broken Cross

WOODLAND interludes and subsidence-induced flashes characterise the Trent & Mersey's serene passage through the Dane Valley. Hereabouts the river (having risen in the Derbyshire Peak District on the flank of Axe Edge - and having been crossed again by Cheshire Ring travellers at Bosley - Map 3) has grown sluggish with age, meandering about its level valley in a series of lazy loops; one moment it's hard by the canal, the next away across the pasturelands of milking herds. The soil here is soft and the Dane carves deep banks made shadowy by alder and willow. The canal shares the valley with a Roman Road known as King Street and a now lightly used railway which once carried a push & pull service between Crewe and Northwich, but these other transport modes barely intrude upon what is otherwise a long, relaxing pound.

The most curious feature of this section of the canal are the flashes bordering the main channel to the south of Bridge 181. That nearest the bridge was once filled with the submerged wrecks of abandoned narrowboats, an inland waterway equivalent of Scapa Flow. Many of the boats were brought here and sunk *en masse* during the Fifties in circumstances as controversial - in canal terms that is - as the scuttling of the German Fleet after the First World War. In what was probably a book-keeping exercise, British Waterways rid themselves of surplus narrowboats in a number of watery graves throughout the system. In recent years the wrecks have been raised and taken off for restoration. One generation's cast-offs become the next's prized possessions.

Whatcroft Hall is topped by a handsome dome. By Bridge 179 its old lodge houses are prettily half-timbered. In the woods between bridges 176 and 177 the mangled remains of old wagon tipplers hint at the existence of clay or puddle pits. Note also how the bridges along this length are flat topped so that they could be relatively easily raised in the event of subsidence.

Croxton Aqueduct was rebuilt to broad-beam dimensions in 1891 so as to permit wide beam craft to work between Anderton and Middlewich. However, after being damaged by flooding in the Thirties, it reverted to its present narrow status.

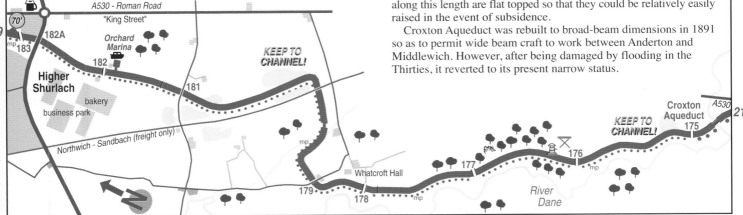

A556 from Altrincham

A530 - Roman Road

"King Street"

19 70'

mp 183 182A

Orchard Marina

182

181

Higher Shurlach

bakery

business park

Northwich - Sandbach (freight only)

KEEP TO CHANNEL!

mp

Whatcroft Hall

179 178 mp

177

River Dane

176

mp

KEEP TO CHANNEL!

Croxton Aqueduct A530 21

175

A556 to Chester   By-road to Davenham

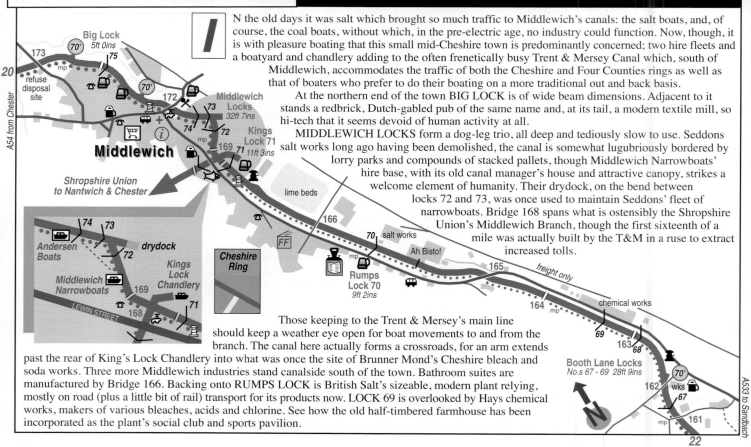

IN the old days it was salt which brought so much traffic to Middlewich's canals: the salt boats, and, of course, the coal boats, without which, in the pre-electric age, no industry could function. Now, though, it is with pleasure boating that this small mid-Cheshire town is predominantly concerned; two hire fleets and a boatyard and chandlery adding to the often frenetically busy Trent & Mersey Canal which, south of Middlewich, accommodates the traffic of both the Cheshire and Four Counties rings as well as that of boaters who prefer to do their boating on a more traditional out and back basis.

At the northern end of the town BIG LOCK is of wide beam dimensions. Adjacent to it stands a redbrick, Dutch-gabled pub of the same name and, at its tail, a modern textile mill, so hi-tech that it seems devoid of human activity at all.

MIDDLEWICH LOCKS form a dog-leg trio, all deep and tediously slow to use. Seddons salt works long ago having been demolished, the canal is somewhat lugubriously bordered by lorry parks and compounds of stacked pallets, though Middlewich Narrowboats' hire base, with its old canal manager's house and attractive canopy, strikes a welcome element of humanity. Their drydock, on the bend between locks 72 and 73, was once used to maintain Seddons' fleet of narrowboats. Bridge 168 spans what is ostensibly the Shropshire Union's Middlewich Branch, though the first sixteenth of a mile was actually built by the T&M in a ruse to extract increased tolls.

Those keeping to the Trent & Mersey's main line should keep a weather eye open for boat movements to and from the branch. The canal here actually forms a crossroads, for an arm extends past the rear of King's Lock Chandlery into what was once the site of Brunner Mond's Cheshire bleach and soda works. Three more Middlewich industries stand canalside south of the town. Bathroom suites are manufactured by Bridge 166. Backing onto RUMPS LOCK is British Salt's sizeable, modern plant relying, mostly on road (plus a little bit of rail) transport for its products now. LOCK 69 is overlooked by Hays chemical works, makers of various bleaches, acids and chlorine. See how the old half-timbered farmhouse has been incorporated as the plant's social club and sports pavilion.

OCKS proliferate, and are potentially habit-forming, as the Trent & Mersey ascends from (or descends to) the Cheshire Plain. There are twenty-six chambers to negotiate in only seven miles between Wheelock and Hardings Wood, and "Heartbreak Hill" - as this section has been known to generations of boaters - seems an all too appropriate nickname by the time you have reached the top or bottom; 250 feet up or down.

With the exception of the PIERPOINT pair, all the locks were 'duplicated' in the 1830s, paddles between adjoining chambers enabling one lock to act as a mini-reservoir to its neighbour. These side paddles were taken out of use when commercial traffic ceased towards the end of the 1960s, but the duplicated locks still ease delays today, as well as offering the opportunity to exchange travellers' tales with boaters operating adjacent chambers.

The locks may, or may not, make life hard for the boater, but the canal itself is illuminated by a succession of small communities with interesting pasts. Sandbach stays a stubborn mile or more out of reach of the canaller, but you can savour the voyage around its outskirts and intermittent views of the tower of its parish church. At ETTILY HEATH the quadrupled, electrified tracks of the Crewe to Manchester railway cross the canal at the site of a transhipment basin provided to facilitate traffic with the Potteries. Hereabouts the canal, concrete-banked and steel-piled, tends to be deeper than is normal on account of subsidence caused by salt-mining in the past. The River Wheelock rises in the vicinity of Little Moreton Hall and gives its name to a former wharfingering community situated where the Crewe-Sandbach road crossed the canal. The village is now by-passed by the aforementioned highway and traffic on the new road thunders across the canal just below Lock 66. MALKIN'S BANK was home to the families of boatmen engaged in comparatively short-haul traffics connected with the salt and chemical industries. They lived cheek-by-jowl with employees at the huge Brunner-Mond sodium carbonate works which is now buried beneath the greens and fairways of Malkins Bank golf course. Between locks 62 and 63, a side bridge carries the towpath over an old arm which once went into the chemical works. Now, happily, it has found a new lease of life with a small boatyard specialising in the maintenance of traditional craft.

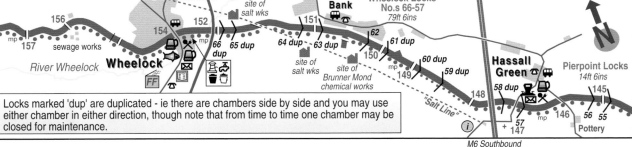

Locks marked 'dup' are duplicated - ie there are chambers side by side and you may use either chamber in either direction, though note that from time to time one chamber may be closed for maintenance.

Middlewich
Map 21

A salt making town since the days of the Roman occupation, Middlewich's most interesting building is the parish church of St Michael whose tower is scarred with missiles unleashed during the Civil War. Leaflets are obtainable from the library to guide you around some of the known sites of Roman history.

BIG LOCK - canalside Big Lock. Big lock, big screen, big portions. Tel: 01606 833489.
KINDERTON'S - hotel/restaurant adjacent Bridge 172. Tel: 01606 834325.
KINGS LOCK - canalside Kings Lock. Food and accommodation. Tel: 01606 833537.
NEWTON BREWERY INN - canalside south of Big Lock. Old fashioned Marston's local. Tel: 01606 833502.
In the town you'll find more baltis than in Bangladesh. BALTI SPICE has the dubious distinction of occupying the once elegant premises of Vernons butchers - Tel: 01606 837030.
Fish & chip shop by Kings Lock.

There's a large Somerfield supermarket just off Wheelock Street, and branches of NatWest and Barclays banks. A small market is held every Tuesday, whilst a number of shops close at midday on Wednesdays.

BUSES - Arriva service 37 links Middlewich with Sandbach and Crewe (for the railway station). Tel: 0870 6082608.

Wheelock
Map 22

Although now by-passed by the A534, Wheelock still endures more than its fair share of traffic - a culture shock after the peace of the canal. Nevertheless, it's a useful pitstop with a newsagent and post office selling canal souvenirs. Refreshment opportunities are plentiful: try the CHESHIRE CHEESE (Tel: 01270 760319), the CAMRA recommended and wonderfully timeless COMMERCIAL HOTEL (Tel: 01270 760122), DI VENEZIA, a wharfside Italian restaurant (Tel: 01270 762030) or STOMPERS excellent fish & chip shop (Tel: 01270 768114. Buses to Crewe and Sandbach. The latter is a fascinating old town, not only for its Saxon crosses but also as an historic centre for the manufacture of lorries.

Hassall Green
Map 22

Isolated community somewhat impinged upon by the M6, though there are still pleasant walks to be had along the neighbouring country lanes. Downhill, past the little mission church painted shocking pink, the old Sandbach branch of the North Staffordshire Railway has been converted into the "Salt Line" bridleway. There's a pottery adjacent to Bridge 146. Refreshments are available at the LOCK 57 CAFE/BRASSERIE (Tel: 01270 762266) or at the ROMPING DONKEY (Tel: 01270 765202), a country pub only a few hundred yards north of Bridge 147. The canalside post office stores sells a good range of canal souvenirs, books, maps etc.

Rode Heath
Map 23

Sizeable modern village at junction of A533 and A50. Two pubs vie for your custom: the BROUGHTON ARMS (Tel: 01270 765202), canalside by Bridge 139, and the ROYAL OAK (Tel: 01270 875670), reached from Bridge 142. Both are popular with boaters. There's also a Chinese takeaway called JADE GARDEN (Tel: 01270 873391), off licence and newsagent/post office. Buses run to and from the Potteries - Tel: 0870 608 2 608.

RODE HALL - 18th century country house and gardens. The house is open to the public on Wednesday afternoons throughout the summer, the grounds additionally on Tuesdays and Thursdays. Teas! Tel: 01270 873237.

Kidsgrove
Map 23

A former colliery town, on the wrong side of Harecastle Hill to qualify as a member of that exclusive hellfire club called The Potteries. Its initially foreboding air can thaw on closer acquaintance. James Brindley is buried at Newchapel, a couple of miles to the east.

BLUE BELL - adjacent Lock 41. Tel: 01782 774052. Award-winning CAMRA recommended pub prized for its ever changing cycle of real ales.
RED BULL - adjacent Lock 43. Tel: 01270 782600. One of Robinsons of Stockport's most southerly outposts. Good food also.

Kiddy's shops are its strong point. They may look dour from the street but within the locals are at their most vital and receptive. London Road suggests, misleadingly, that it is the heart of the place, but the real centre lies a stone's throw to the north and even boasts a small market on Tuesdays. Here, also, you will find Tesco and KwikSave supermarkets, butchers, bakers and branches of the main banks and a launderette. Make it your goal to find BRENDA'S where you can watch oatcakes and pikelets, those twin bastions of North Staffordshire gastronomy, being freshly made on the griddle, and have your oatcakes crammed with a choice of nourishing fillings. Calor gas and solid fuel are obtainable from SMITHSONS by Bridge 132.

BUSES - frequent services throughout the area. Tel: 01782 207999.
TRAINS - useful (though limited to peak hours) service northwards through Congleton and Macclesfield. Better served, is Stoke-on-Trent, a ten minute ride away, where connections are available to London, Birmingham and the rest of the known world. Tel: 08457 484950.

ONE hardly knows where to begin describing this richly rewarding and entertaining length of the Trent & Mersey Canal as it continues its passage through the long line of 'Cheshire Locks'. All the locks were duplicated under the direction of Thomas Telford in the 1830s; though one or two have since been singled.

Lawton 'Treble' Locks are Telford's work and replaced a Brindley staircase, both time-consuming and wasteful of water. Beyond Church Locks there is a brief respite from the locks and the pleasant sight of Lawton church beside the woods surrounding Lawton Hall. Throughout this length the countryside dips and sweeps away from the canal in folds and creases like a carelessly discarded garment, revealing lush pastures interrupted by pockets of woodland through which footpaths beckon enticingly.

Red Bull Locks - once individually called Townfield, Kent's and Yewtree in order of ascent - are probably the most visually satisfying on the whole of 'Heartbreak Hill'. All the elements are there by happy accident: a long, low stone wall separates the towpath from fields sloping down to the A50 edged by Lawton Woods; the

sweeping symmetries of the paired chambers masked from the railway by a high bank of beech trees; and an old whitewashed warehouse once used for the storage of perishable goods.

Pool Lock Aqueduct seems weighed down by the responsibility of carrying what is now commonly referred to as the Macclesfield Canal over the Trent & Mersey. Pedants will tell you that the upper canal is not really the Macclesfield because - as discussed on Map 1 - it was the Trent & Mersey themselves who built the Hall Green Branch. Oddly, though, Bridge 98 at HARDINGS WOOD JUNCTION incorporates an inscription stone proclaiming "Macclesfield Canal MDCCCXXVIIII", so perhaps the Trent & Mersey were not such malcontents after all.

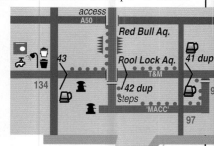

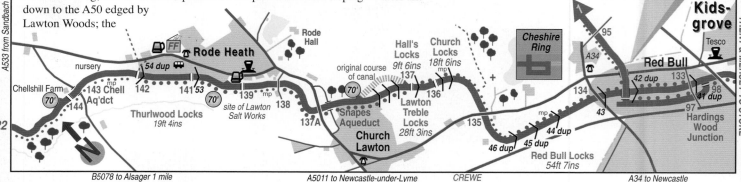

The

The RUFFORD & RIBBLE Routes

WORSLEY is where it all began. The Duke of Bridgewater's canal to Stretford was the Stockton & Darlington of the Canal Age. It opened in 1761 and included an aqueduct over the Irwell at Barton which Brindley modelled in cheese in a demonstration before incredulous Members of Parliament. You would have thought they'd have taken Mr B at his word by then, after all he'd made mud pies in the House of Commons to prove that canal water wouldn't leak.

At Worsley the canal was linked with a network of subterranean waterways leading to the coal faces of the Duke's mines. Later a second level of underground canal developed, astonishingly connected to the main level by an inclined plane. Subsequently, a third level was added and, at its zenith, the underground system of canals totalled over forty miles.

A special type of boat evolved for the carriage of coal which, because of their narrow lines and the fact that their ribs showed, became known as Starvationers. Ingeniously, they were propelled from the coal face by the opening of a sluice gate which created an artificial current. Surfacing at The Delph, through a portal still visible to this day, they were towed three abreast by pairs of horses to Manchester.

All that activity belongs to another age. Worsley is a leafy residential suburb now, seeming introspectively to mull over its more colourful past; a Field Marshal with no more battles to fight, a canal without any trade more pressing to carry than the holiday boats of the Leisure Age.

So people come to Worsley

Boothshall Bridge

Hollins Wood

Bittern Pits Wood

Bridgewater Marina

B5211 from Stretford

Trafford Centre

ASDA

Ashburton Road Bridge

Barton Swing Aqueduct

A57 from Warrington

Barton Upon Irwell

50'

Patricroft Br.

Worsley Cruising Club

70'

Patricroft

12

BARTON ROAD

granary

wc

P

drydocks

monument

boat house

Packet House

old mines

Worsley Br.

Worsley

Junct. 13

MANCHESTER SHIP CANAL

The Barge

Irwell Park Wharf

Monton Green Br.

Monton

golf course

A572 to Leigh

N

M602 to Salford   A57 to Manchester   A572 to Swinton   M60   A575 to Farnworth

Barton Swing Aqueduct

now, like Victoria did in 1851 aboard a packet from Patricroft, simply for the pleasure of doing so. To gongoozle the colourful boats, to feed the geese, to take snapshots of the peculiarly orange water (caused by ironstone leaching - just as at Kidsgrove - from the old mines), or to catch the trip boat from the very steps, beside the half-timbered Packet House, down which canal passengers of two centuries ago descended to board the packets for Wigan and Manchester.

At Barton, Brindley's 'canal in the air' was superseded in 1894 by Leader-Williams' swing aqueduct. Vessels using the Ship Canal required more headroom than the original masonry arches could offer, so the new bridge was designed as a moveable caisson of water which could be manoeuvred to facilitate passage along the new waterway. It swings to this day - along with the adjacent road bridge - but less frequently now that trade on the upper reaches of the Manchester Ship Canal is just a pale shadow of its heyday.

Passing through Patricroft, the Bridgewater Canal passes beneath Stephenson's Liverpool & Manchester Railway, scene of the Rocket's triumph in 1829. At the other end of steam power's reign, Patricroft motive power depot was one of the last surviving engine sheds still catering for steam locomotives before their official withdrawal in 1968. Locomotives, for overseas customers as far flung as Japan, were built at Nasmyth's foundry which later became an Ordnance Works. Some handsome textile mills overlook the canal and must once have kept it busy. One of them now houses a large home shopping by catalogue business which includes a bargain shop that the female of the species may enjoy visiting. More likely, they'll be drawn to the Trafford Centre, a massive shopping complex along the lines of Bluewater or Meadowhall.

In 1795 the Duke secured an Act to extend his canal northwards from Worsley to Leigh in order to forge a link with the mighty Leeds & Liverpool. Nowadays this route reflects ample evidence of former mining as it wends its way above the flat landscape which, over the years, has sunk around it. From its superior elevation there are vistas southwards across the wild mosslands to the distant chemical works at Partington, and north towards the Pennine hills. Adjacent to Boothshall Bridge, a former colliery basin has been adapted as a mooring lagoon beside a new pub, and plays host to Bridgewater Marina.

O LD colliery basins abound on this length of the Bridgewater Canal, and it bears remembering that barges conveyed coal from mines along here to Trafford Park power station until 1972. But thirty years of neglect and decay have taken their toll of both the coal mining and water transport industries. Only the skeletal headstock of a former mine at Astley Green recalls the hurly burly of the past, at the same time emphasising the desolation of the present. Fortunately this particular mine is the object of a preservation group's loving attention and is now open to the public on several afternoons.

Nevertheless, one would dearly liked to have seen this landscape when it worked for a living; before it acquired the melancholy sonority of a brass band. It would have been fascinating to pass this way when colliery engines were still puffing and panting across the fields with trains of protesting wagons on tortuous tracks to basin-side tipplers, where their contents would be summarily upended and shot into the black holds of waiting 'Wiganers'. And at a shift's end, it would have been an education to encounter mine-workers trudging home along the towpath, too tired to bother avoiding the boat-horses' dung, too blackened by coal dust for their faces to be recognised in the South Lancashire dusk.

ASTLEY GREEN is a worthwhile mooring point, what with its pair of pubs (one with etched glass windows proclaiming the bar known as the 'News Room' - "Aye lads, Nat's got another hat trick for t'Wanderers" - fish & chip shop and bus link with civilisation. Half an hour's stroll to the south along 'Rindle Road' will bring you to the wastes of Chat Moss where Stephenson was forced to lay his railway tracks on floating bundles of faggots to prevent the new iron way from sinking into the bog.

Morley's Bridge carries the East Lancs Road - synonymous, for some, with the 1960s TV series "Z Cars", or, for the more intellectual, with the poetry of Adrian Henri - across the canal on a skew.

At BEDFORD, on the outskirts of Leigh, coal gave way to cotton. Vast textile mills still border the canal with domed towers glinting like mosques in the pale Lancashire daylight. Pride is emblazoned on every date-stamped edifice - LEIGH SPINNERS, LEIGH MANUFACTURING CO., BUTTS MILL, BROOKLANDS MILL - built to last for ever, but now outlasting their usefulness; though you can still eavesdrop on the earthy banter of latter-day mill girls in the fish bar by Butt's Bridge. "Ee, 'e never did, did 'e?"

Map labels:

Boothstown Bridge
Vicars Hall Bridge
Whitehead Hall Bridge
By-road from Chat Moss
24
70'
N
Astley Green Colliery
Astley Bridge
Lingard's Foot Bridge
Astley Green
EAST LANCS ROAD
A580
Morley's Bridge
70'
Marsland Green Br.
Great Fold Br.
Town Lane
Marsland Green
school
Hall House Br.
Butt's Bridge
mills
Bedford
mills
FF
A5/2 to Warrington
2
A578 to Leigh

**Canalside scenes at Leigh
on the Bridgewater Canal**

55

IMPERCEPTIBLY the Bridgewater Canal gives way to the Leeds & Liverpool at Leigh Bridge and once again you are back in the capable hands of British Waterways. A former warehouse overlooking the Leeds & Liverpool side of the frontier is enjoying a new lease of life as the 'Waterside Inn', but not so fortunate was Mansley's ropeworks which stood beside the towpath. The ropeworks burnt down in 1981, having been in business for a century and a half, and the site is now occupied by modern housing. The works' canalside location in Leigh was not accidental. Waste cotton yarn from local mills was woven into 'warps' and then twisted into strands on the ropewalk to produce the finished article. Boat companies were amongst Mansley's biggest customers.

West of Leigh, the Leeds & Liverpool Canal's Leigh Branch negotiates a neighbourhood once given over almost entirely to coal mining. A dense network of railway lines either crossed the canal or came to an abrupt, yet supremely functional, end at one colliery basin or another. Bickershaw Colliery, at Plank Lane, was the last local mine to close in 1992. Earlier editions of this guide recalled how wide boats carried coal from Plank Lane to Wigan's Westwood Power Station until as comparatively recently as 1972.

Even in our time we watched Class 20 hauled coal trains creeping hesitantly down rickety tracks with consignments of coal for more distant power plants. All of which leaves the present, however green again, just a tad devoid of character. Now that the mines are just a memory, an overwhelming loneliness pervades the landscape. Herons flap over sedge fringed flashes, figures mooch disconsolately over wastegrounds, and Pennington Flash glitters prettily with sailing dinghies as if this was suddenly the South of France.

PLANK LANE LIFT BRIDGE is a mechanised structure operated by a British Waterways keeper (Tel: 01925 847700 for times). His job would not appear to be overly stressful, there being no more than half a dozen craft a day passing this way on most days. Plenty of time left for touching up the immaculately kept bridge girders!

In the vicinity of Crankwood steep banks indicate just how far subsidence has caused the land beside the canal to sink. The disappearance of two locks at Dover also indicates the change of levels that has occurred, as does the unusual depth of the canal along this section.

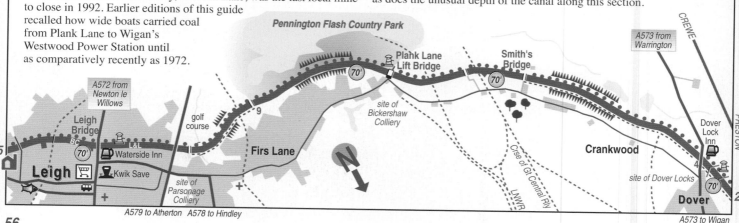

Worsley
Map 24

Half-timbered houses and broad swards of grass ensure that Worsley attracts land and water-based visitors alike. St Mark's Church chimes 13 at 1pm! There are lots of pleasant strolls to be had beside the orange-tinged canal, whilst here and there interpretive boards outline the village's busy commercial past. Indeed, with a bit of spare fat on your Cheshire Ring schedule, Worsley makes a worthwhile detour up from Water's Meeting, perhaps for an overnight stay.

MILAN - adjacent to canal in village centre. Italian restaurant. Good food and atmosphere. Tel: 0161 794 5444.

JJ's - restaurant close to old mines entrance. Tel: 0161 793 6003.

TUNG FONG - as above. Attractive Chinese restaurant. Tel: 0161 794 5331.

Plus a couple of highly popular pubs.

Shopping facilities are somewhat surprisingly limited to a small newsagents. Presumably the natives all go to the beastly Trafford Centre now.

BUSES - Regular services to/from Manchester, Leigh and Wigan of particular value to towpath walkers. Tel: 0161 228 7811.

Astley Green
Map 25

Former mining community with two pubs, the OLD BOATHOUSE (Tel: 01942 883300) and the ROSS'S ARMS (01942 874405), as well as a fish & chip shop. A bus service provides a link with the outside world. ASTLEY GREEN COLLIERY MUSEUM is open Sunday, Tuesday and Thursday afternoons throughout the year. The mine closed in 1970 but the massive headgear haunts the horizon still, the last of its iconic kind in Lancashire. Another survival is the Yates & Thom winding engine, all 3,300hp of it. And why is it the entrance gates remind you so forcibly of Willy Wonka!

Leigh
Map 26

A surprisingly substantial town which has a longer pedigree than its prevailing image of a mill and mine community implies. The noble town hall dates from 1907 and is, according to the local publicity handout, "a dignified expression of civic prosperity and pride." Nearby, the modern library boasts an interior fish pond and, it must be said, an excellent local history section; just the thing for itinerant guide book compilers. James Hilton, author of *Goodbye Mr Chips, Lost Horizon* and *Random Harvest* - all novels turned into notable movies in the golden age of Hollywood - was born in Leigh. The atmosphere of a northern industrial town pervades one of his less well known works, *So Well Remembered,* but the local tourist authority haven't, as yet, turned this into 'Hilton Country', so perhaps he's not *that* 'well remembered'!

On a more practical level, the town centre and all its facilities lies just north of Leigh Bridge, by which there are ample moorings, if occasionally disturbingly haunted by local youths. The WATERSIDE INN features in CAMRA's *Good Beer Guide* (Tel: 01942 605005) or you could try the BELLA BISTRO on Railway Road (off King Street) Tel: 01942 269279. There is no longer a railway station, but frequent buses link Leigh with Wigan and Manchester (Tel: 0161-228 7811) but oh for a sight of a South Lancs trolleybus!

Dover
Map 26

No white cliffs at this Dover, a typical East Lancs mining village. There is a canalside pub, however, named the DOVER LOCK INN (Tel: 01942 866300) after the vanished locks which were a victim of subsidence.

THE canal traveller's 'Road to Wigan Pier' traverses a much wounded landscape where the scar tissue of old mines and ironworks has yet to fully heal. A sort of inverted archipelago of subsidence induced lakes, or flashes, lines the canal, bearing peculiar comparison with the Shropshire meres that border the altogether more picturesque Llangollen Canal.

Between 1930 and 1958 Bridge 3 carried the wires of the South Lancashire Transport trolleybus route across the canal. Totalling more than 35 route miles, and linking such disparate industrial communities as Ashton-in-Makerfield, Hindley, Leigh, Swinton, Farnworth and Bolton, the company's fleet was notable for the longevity of its vehicles, a number of its six-wheel, Roe bodied Guys remaining in use for the whole span of the operation.

Overhead wires do, however, hang above the railway tracks of the West Coast Main Line where it bridges the canal adjacent to the site of Bamfurlong Colliery, now just a wasteground of scrub. A succession of rusted wagon tipplers point to where coal was loaded onto boats in days gone by. Between Bamfurlong and Poolstock no roads, nor any houses, come remotely near the canal. On the skyline ahead, Wigan rises up

like an industrial Lindisfarne and you feel you are travelling towards it across the quicksands of time.

POOLSTOCK LOCKS bring one abruptly back to reality. To thwart the hooligans, who would otherwise derive some obscure enjoyment from letting the pounds run dry, the paddle gear is 'locked', and you will need the sort of key you probably encountered back on the Ashton Canal to undo it. These wide beam locks, and those between the Leigh Branch Junction and Liverpool, are long enough to accept a full length narrowboat; Leeds & Liverpool locks east of Wigan being only 62ft in length.

Just beyond Poolstock locks the main line of the Leeds & Liverpool Canal is encountered. To the right, on land now occupied by building society offices, stood Westwood Power Station, where the last cargoes of coal were delivered by barge

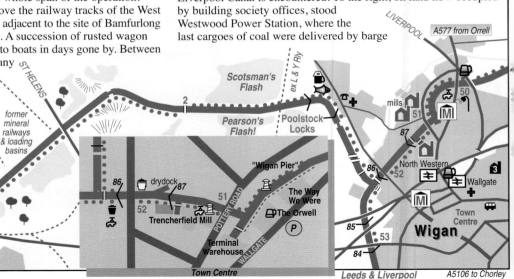

in 1972. A ladder of twenty-one locks carries the canal up around Wigan on its Trans Pennine journey over to Yorkshire as depicted in our *Pennine Waters Canal Companion*.

But in this guide we turn left for Wigan Pier, negotiating two more locks, the first of which is overlooked by the lock-keeper's house and has water, sanitary station and rubbish disposal facilities to hand. Windlass operated winches open and close the bottom gates which are too close to the adjoining road bridge for balance beams to be provided.

Wigan Pier

Liverpool, opened in 1777, and was connected by tramway to a series of collieries lying southwest of the town.

The pier and its tippler projected from a slightly raised section of towpath. In its heyday 50,000 tons of coal per annum was being transhipped from wagon to barge here, much of it going in export to Ireland, or even America, via Liverpool docks. The collieries, however, were largely worked out after the General Strike and the tippler

The myth and reality of Wigan Pier are inextricably linked. The fact that ugly, landlocked Wigan should have a pier at all appealed to the caustic wit of the locals, and George Formby Senior is credited with popularising the joke in his appearances in the music halls. However, as travellers from Leigh have already seen, the canal banks around Wigan were punctuated at frequent intervals by landing stages for tipping coal wagons, and these were generally regarded as 'piers', even if they failed to conform with the accepted image of the seaside funfair. One pier in particular came to be regarded as the 'Wigan Pier'. It overlooked the basin near the original terminus of the canal from

was dismantled in 1929. Subsequently the pier faded into folklore. George Orwell failed to find it when writing his book in 1936, but at least its publication succeeded in carrying on the tradition of Wigan having a pier. Canal transport ceased at this end of the Leeds & Liverpool Canal in the early Sixties. Wigan Metropolitan Borough Council came up with the bright idea of revitalising the area as a heritage trail. As an exercise in celebrating the past, Wigan Pier and its visitor attractions have proved remarkably successful, but even nostalgia needs updating from time to time, and various aspects of the complex are in the course of being upgraded, with a target date for completion in 2007.

The Leeds & Liverpool Canal at Crooke

WE were not in a fact-finding mood leaving Wigan. Facts are inclined to frog march through the gossamer strands of atmosphere, and the Leeds & Liverpool west of Wigan (historically intertwined with the Douglas Navigation) is nothing if not atmospheric. On a hot July day the towpath was busy but the canal was not. Flaunting bye-laws, there were more children swimming in PAGEFIELD LOCK than boats attempting to use it. Pagefield Ironworks had once belonged to Walkers, manufacturers, amongst other more mundane engineering items, of dainty diesel railcars for the West Clare and County Donegal narrow-gauge railways in Ireland. On our most recent journey Wigan FC, who play at the imposing JJB stadium, had been promoted to the Premiership.

Drifting down the Douglas Valley, we left Wigan's post-industrial periphery behind us, soon finding ourselves in bosky countryside, which even the motorway's high-columned crossing at Gathurst failed to compromise. Arrowhead flourished in one margin, butterbur in the other. In close attendance, and overhung with alder, the Douglas wound between balsamy banks, defying belief that it had once been navigable. But the history books are full of this phenomenon, indicating that the Douglas was carrying coastal sailing flats up through thirteen locks from the Ribble

estuary to Wigan by 1742, three years before Bonnie Prince Charlie lodged in the town and thirty years before the canal linked Wigan with Liverpool.

Here and there are hints that the valley has not always been so rural. Crooke was a centre for mining, and an old arm serves as moorings now where wide boats once loaded coal from John Pit Colliery, much of the area's output travelling west to feed Liverpool's coal-hungry industries. Another source of traffic for the canal was the explosive works at Gathurst. Today the neighbourhood is dominated by Heinz's huge factory on the hillside, but baked beans - more's the pity - don't get carried by barge. Lying in the early morning shadow of the M6 viaduct, Dean Lock was duplicated. At the tail of the locks there is evidence of a connection which once linked with the Douglas. By Bridge 44 a faded plaque recalls that this length won a prize for its piling in 1958!

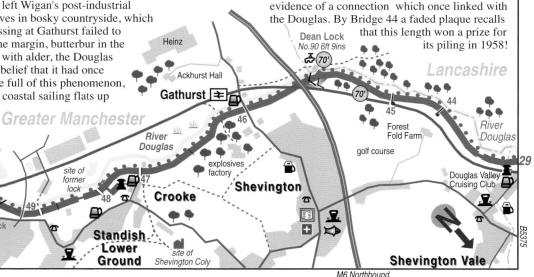

ACCOMPANIED by the River Douglas and the Wigan-Southport railway, the canal slips between two hills whose modest stature is increased in significance by the relatively flat nature of the surrounding landscape. Ashurst's Beacon rises above the treetops to the south. It was erected to warn of French invasion during the Napoleonic wars. Skelmersdale new town lurks over the horizon, source of the little River Tawd; origin, possibly, of the adjective tawdry? Ironically, only the original deep lock at APPLEY BRIDGE is in use. The two shallower chambers, judging by a nailed plank over the top mitres, long abandoned.

An old windmill overlooks the wharf at PARBOLD. Ainscough's of Burscough also had a flour mill on the opposite bank on a site now occupied by housing. Nearby, the canal bends into a strange apex formed of a drydock. The original 'Parliamentary' route of the Leeds & Liverpool Canal was to have led northwards from here, around the flank of Parbold Hill, by-passing Wigan, Chorley and Blackburn altogether.

West of PARBOLD the canal crosses the Douglas, and a lengthy embankment carries it across two country lanes, one of which leads to the pleasant village of Newburgh, scene of much swashbuckling during the Civil War. Swingbridge No.36 is electrified, access to its control panel being by way of BW's standard Yale key. Hereabouts an extensive sewage plant introduces an element of malodorousness into the atmosphere. Pill boxes pop up at strategic intervals alongside the canal. Security was tight here during the Second World War as secret tests were undertaken to ascertain the suitability of raw sewage as a rocket fuel. Sadly, as far as the top brass (brought to Hoscar's remote station by special train for the initial demonstration) were concerned, the plans - quite literally - backfired, leaving one much bespattered French general to remark: "C'est magnifique, mais ce n'est pas la guerre."

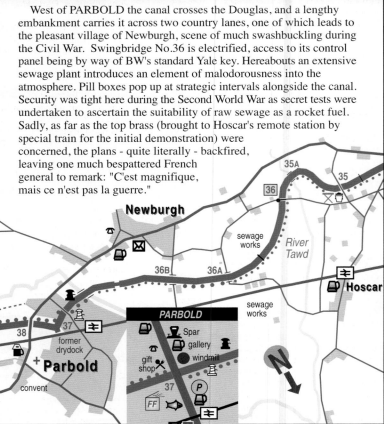

Wigan *Map 27*

Terracotta and concrete collide as, with one foot firmly in the past, Wigan attempts to shed its unwanted and unwarranted Orwellian legacy. But the sheer warmth and good humour of Wigan folk (and their lovely dialect) transcends such a reactionary outlook, and you go back to your boat happy in the knowledge that you have brushed shoulders with a 'real' town and one with its own unique flavour.

THE ORWELL - canalside at Wigan Pier. Warehouse conversion offering lunches and a range of real ales. Tel: 01942 323034.
SWAN & RAILWAY - Wallgate (opposite North Western station). CAMRA recommended, unspoilt town pub with notable mosaic floor. Banks's beers and guest ales. Lunches. Tel: 01942 495032.
CROOKE HALL INN - canalside Bridge 47 (Map 28). Food, garden, moorings. Tel: 01942 247524.
THE NAVIGATION - Bridge 46 (Gathurst - Map 28). Tel: 01257 252856. Friendly canalside pub where you can relax over a game of boules washed down with Taylor's ambrosial Landlord bitter. Home made food too.

The town centre is 5-10 minutes walk from Wigan Pier. Chain stores at THE GALLERIES, more individual retailers at the MARKET HALL.

TOURIST INFORMATION - Wallgate. Tel: 01942-825677.
WIGAN PIER - open every day except Friday throughout the year. Admission charge. Tel: 01942 323666. Popular visitor centre imaginatively relating the story of Wigan's industrial past. Under redevelopment but still open to the public.
THE HISTORY SHOP - Library Street. Open daily except Sat pm and Sun. Admission free. Tel: 01942 828128. Exceptionally fine local history centre based in Victorian library. Museum and heritage displays. Gift shop and art gallery.

TRAINS - services from Wallgate along Douglas Valley corridor to/from Gathurst, Appley Bridge, Parbold and Burscough. Also to Manchester. InterCity services from North Western. Tel: 08457 484950.
BUSES - services throughout the region. Useful links with Leigh in absence of train service. Tel: 0161 228 7811.
TAXIS - Aristacars. Tel: 01942 235235.

Parbold *Map 29*

A thriving, attractive village, not so much in the parts of its individual buildings, but in the sum of its setting. Parbold Hill, a steep half mile to the east of the village, offers panoramic views over the Douglas Valley.

THE WINDMILL - adjacent to Bridge 37. Popular whitewashed pub offering meals both sessions. Tel: 01257 464130.
Chinese fish & chips and Indian takeaway plus tea room in gift shop.

Good range of shops within easy reach of Bridge 37 including a small SOMER-FIELD, chemist and delicatessen (which does good fresh sandwiches etc) as well as a branch of the Royal Bank of Scotland (with cash machine).

TRAINS - station handy to canal. Local services to/from Southport, Burscough Bridge, Wigan etc. Tel: 08457 484950.

Burscough Bridge *Map 30*

Useful facilities for passing boaters, including a newsagent, baker, butcher (proudly boasting of "Syd's award winning pies"), delicatessen, pharmacy, a couple of supermarkets, branches of several banks, and there are fish & chip shops and ethnic takeaways too. Close by the junction of the Main Line and Rufford Arm, the SHIP INN (Tel: 01704 893117) is a popular pub where meals are served daily. It has a pleasant little garden with fine views of the surrounding countryside. From the Bridge railway station trains run to Southport (a worthwhile excursion for boaters) and Wigan (useful for one-way towpath walkers) Tel: 08457 484950.

Rufford *Map 30*

A straggling village strung out along the old Preston-Liverpool turnpike. Local trains run to Preston and Ormskirk - Tel: 08457 484950.

FETTLERS WHARF - Cosy marina coffee shop open daily from 9am to 5pm. Home made food, anything from a jam scone to a plate of fish & chips. Tel: 01704 822888.

RUFFORD OLD HALL - canalside, though official access via entrance on A59. Open April-October Saturday to Wednesday. House 1-5pm; gardens, shop and tearoom from 12 noon. Gardens also open weekends Nov and Dec. Admission charge. Tel: 01704 821254. Sublime sixteenth century house preserved by National Trust in eighteen acres of gardens and woodland. The cakes in the tea room are sumptuous!

Tarleton *Map 31*

Though the village itself is largely nondescript, it nevertheless offers a reassuring sense of civilisation in the wastes which surround the Douglas's descent to the sea. Pubs and fish & chips aplenty. Tarleton has a surprisingly good range of shops as well, including a chemist, butcher, delicatessen (offering barbecued chickens), bakery, off licence, Spar, Co-op supermarket and a branch of NatWest bank with cash machine. Arriva buses run to/from Preston and Ormskirk - Tel: 0870 608 2 608.

AS canal junctions go, the one at Burscough ("Bursco" in the vernacular) is not one of the busiest, best known or most picturesque on the inland waterway system. It does, however, present the canal traveller with a stark choice: either continue along the Main Line of the L&L for a further twenty-five miles to its western terminus in Merseyside's docklands, or turn aside to explore the esoteric charms of the RUFFORD BRANCH, a

seven mile canal down to the River Douglas and beyond to the Ribble Link and the Lancaster Canal, recently connected with the rest of the inland waterways network for the first time in its existence. It would indeed be fun to continue into Liverpool, where we could catch a game at Anfield or Goodison, visit the Merseyside Maritime Museum and take a stroll along Penny Lane, but sadly we lack sufficient space to do justice to that stimulating canal journey. Instead, therefore, we turn our attention to the delights of the Rufford Branch, opened in 1781 to improve the facilities for exporting Wigan's coal. Before heading north, however, boaters may care to avail themselves of the facilities (banks, shops etc) at Burscough Bridge but it is advisable to leave craft in excess of 50ft at the Junction, there being no winding hole at Burscough Wharf.

BURSCOUGH JUNCTION itself is a canal community in microcosm, with canal workers' cottages, a drydock which looks as if it has been 'on the wagon' for a good many years, and an old (but much refurbished) boatmen's pub once known as the 'Blood Bucket', but now, more respectably, as the "Ship Inn". Once 60% of Burscough's working population was

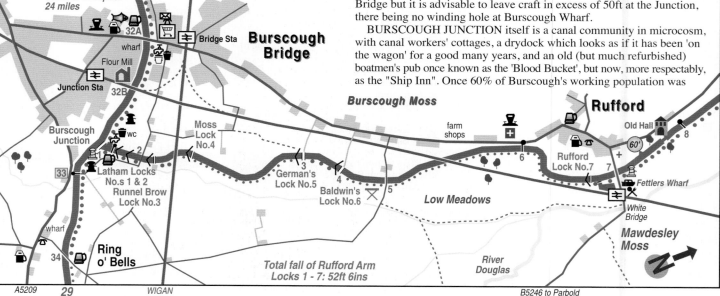

64

engaged in canal related employment: from the craftsmen of two boatbuilding yards, to the men who had the noisome task of unloading Liverpool's 'night soil' (used as manure by the local farms) at Ring O'Bells Wharf.

Passing down through a series of broad (but only 62ft long) locks, the branch rapidly establishes a rural atmosphere, traversing a flat landscape reclaimed from marshland early in the 18th century, and largely given over to market gardening, its peaty soil providing a perfect loam. The cut's broad margins are colonised by reed, iris, arrowhead and water lily; the banks burgeon with willowherb, bindweed and bracken. Larks sing overhead whilst coots and moorhens inhabit the reed beds. An ambivalent 'world's end' demeanour imposes itself upon the canal traveller. Distant vegetable pickers in the fields appear ephemeral, but it was their eighteenth century ancestors who bequeathed their names to the locks and bridges along this length of canal. Potato crops are a significant part of the local agricultural economy. Their cultivation hereabouts dates back to the middle of the nineteenth century when the local entrepreneur, James Martland, founder of the Potato Merchants Steamship Company, was proclaimed 'potato king of the world'. Nearing picking time, the potato plants sprout cream or violet coloured flowers. Similarly, the Rufford Arm's locks sprout all sorts of weird, wonderful, and generally user friendly paddle gear, including a number of cloughs. But it seems sad that the top paddles, and indeed some of the swing-bridges, need to be handcuff-locked in what is ostensibly a remote region.

The Ormskirk-Preston railway accompanies the canal, once an important route of the old Lancashire & Yorkshire Railway, but now a single track byway with a shuttle service of single unit railcars offering an entertaining excursion 'ashore' across the flatlands to the fleshpots of Preston. At Rufford's remote and riverine station the trains' drivers exchange wooden 'staffs' and hooped 'tokens' with the crossing-keeper. The village of Rufford, which lends the arm its name, lies about halfway along its course. An isolated lock stands out in the fields near the station, beyond which an old stone bridge carries the B road to Parbold over the Douglas, a high, balsamy-banked imposter of a Fenland drain. A new marina here has brought much extra - and welcome - traffic to the arm. Rufford Old Hall, now an engaging National Trust property, was reputedly visited by Shakespeare.

*T*HE branch's mysterious character deepens. Market gardening gives way to wider, prairie-like expanses of cornfield and grassland. In some ways it reminds you of the Chelmer & Blackwater Navigation in Essex, another little known waterway which also builds to an estuarial climax.

At SOLLOM - which is too pretty a hamlet (devoted to race horse training) to live up to the sound of its name - the canal gives up all attempt to continue impersonating a man-made waterway, and joins the original course of the Douglas river beyond the narrows of a former lock chamber.

Winding this way and that between swaying reed-beds, one half expects an arm to rise out of the water waving Excalibur. At Bank Hall an old warehouse presides over the branch and the busy A59 Preston-Liverpool road crosses. Nearby stands Bank Hall, a decaying mansion which appeared on BBC's *Restoration*.

Prior to creation of the Millennium Ribble Link, the Rufford Arm petered out at Tarleton, few boaters having the desire, yet alone experience, to lock down into the tidal Douglas. The MRL opened in 2002 in belated response to two centuries delay in connecting the Lancaster

Canal to the rest of the inland waterways network. Most of the almost £6 million cost was involved in upgrading Savick Brook to navigable standard, including the construction of nine locks. Savick Brook links the Lancaster Canal to the tidal River Ribble. The River Douglas links the Rufford Arm of the Leeds & Liverpool Canal with the Ribble.

Voyages between the Rufford Arm at Tarleton and the Lancaster Canal on the outskirts of Preston are strictly controlled by British Waterways. Convoys of pre-booked inland waterway craft (Tel: 01925 847700) make the journey in one direction only on days selected to coincide with favourable tidal conditions in the two rivers. Hire boats are not usually permitted to make the journey, whilst privately owned craft have to comply with safety conditions - anchors, life jackets (for all crew members) and mobile phones etc are mandatory. Such stringencies notwithstanding, the passage between the two canals has rapidly become recognised by experienced boaters as one of the most adventurous and enjoyable itineraries currently available.

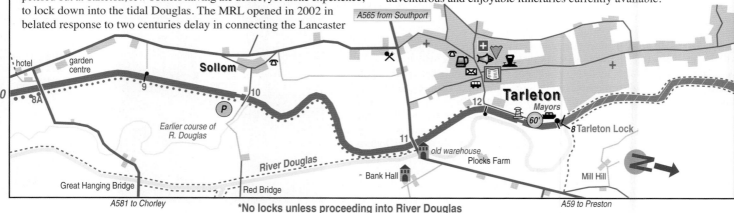

*No locks unless proceeding into River Douglas

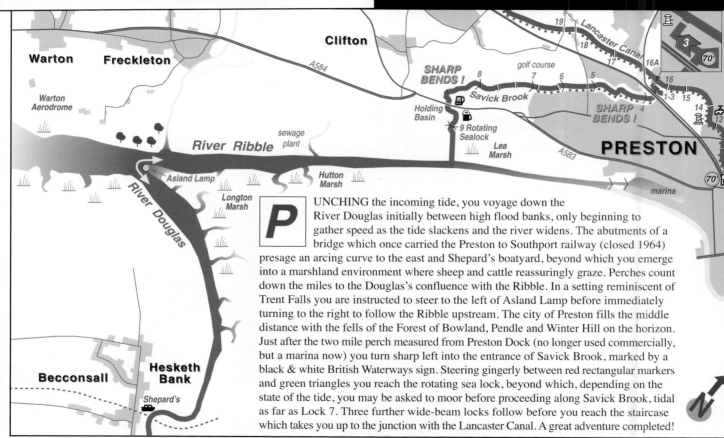

PUNCHING the incoming tide, you voyage down the River Douglas initially between high flood banks, only beginning to gather speed as the tide slackens and the river widens. The abutments of a bridge which once carried the Preston to Southport railway (closed 1964) presage an arcing curve to the east and Shepard's boatyard, beyond which you emerge into a marshland environment where sheep and cattle reassuringly graze. Perches count down the miles to the Douglas's confluence with the Ribble. In a setting reminiscent of Trent Falls you are instructed to steer to the left of Asland Lamp before immediately turning to the right to follow the Ribble upstream. The city of Preston fills the middle distance with the fells of the Forest of Bowland, Pendle and Winter Hill on the horizon. Just after the two mile perch measured from Preston Dock (no longer used commercially, but a marina now) you turn sharp left into the entrance of Savick Brook, marked by a black & white British Waterways sign. Steering gingerly between red rectangular markers and green triangles you reach the rotating sea lock, beyond which, depending on the state of the tide, you may be asked to moor before proceeding along Savick Brook, tidal as far as Lock 7. Three further wide-beam locks follow before you reach the staircase which takes you up to the junction with the Lancaster Canal. A great adventure completed!

31

Please note that this map is to a reduced scale of 1 inch to 1 mile

The **WEAVER** Navigation

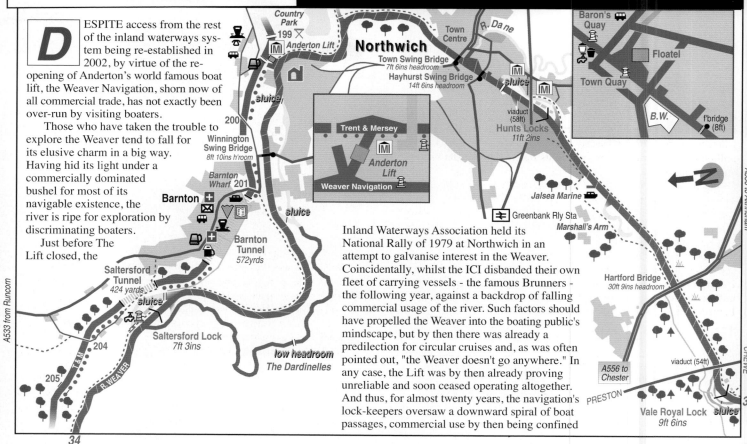

DESPITE access from the rest of the inland waterways system being re-established in 2002, by virtue of the re-opening of Anderton's world famous boat lift, the Weaver Navigation, shorn now of all commercial trade, has not exactly been over-run by visiting boaters.

Those who have taken the trouble to explore the Weaver tend to fall for its elusive charm in a big way. Having hid its light under a commercially dominated bushel for most of its navigable existence, the river is ripe for exploration by discriminating boaters.

Just before The Lift closed, the

Inland Waterways Association held its National Rally of 1979 at Northwich in an attempt to galvanise interest in the Weaver. Coincidentally, whilst the ICI disbanded their own fleet of carrying vessels - the famous Brunners - the following year, against a backdrop of falling commercial usage of the river. Such factors should have propelled the Weaver into the boating public's mindscape, but by then there was already a predilection for circular cruises and, as was often pointed out, "the Weaver doesn't go anywhere." In any case, the Lift was by then already proving unreliable and soon ceased operating altogether. And thus, for almost twenty years, the navigation's lock-keepers oversaw a downward spiral of boat passages, commercial use by then being confined to the weekly appearance of a coaster carrying calcium chloride from Winnington to Ayr or Girvan.

Upstream

In a way The Lift is reminiscent of the Tees Transporter Bridge at Middlesbrough, combining that same mixture of Victorian ingenuity and incredulity. A cliff railway is another analogy which springs to mind. Facts? The lift dates from 1875 and was designed by Edwin Clark. Its framework contains two water-filled caissons, each capable of holding a pair of narrowboats. Corrosion of the metalwork brought about closure in 1983. Years of uncertainty and frustration followed before rebuilding commenced in 2000 with Heritage Lottery Funding. Two years and £7 million later, Anderton Lift re-opened its watery doors, a star visitor attraction in its own right, nevermind its usefulness.

Boaters wishing to use the Lift to reach the Weaver from the Trent & Mersey may do so free of charge but it is advisable to pre-book (for which there is a small fee!) by telephoning British Waterways on 01606 786777. The sense of expectation is high, adventure palpable, as you make your way into one or other of the caissons. It looks a long way down, the machinery menacing, but in truth the journey itself is ever so slightly something of an anti-climax; a conjuring show without a rabbit in the hat. Better, perhaps, to let the river 'weave' its own particular magic. Turning upstream, it seems enormously wide by Trent & Mersey standards. Immediately the Weaver's characteristically self-effacing style manifests itself, high banks emphasising the river's solitary disposition.

Presently, Northwich town centre begins to make its presence felt on the left bank. Casual mooring is recommended at Baron's Quay. Opposite are water, sanitary station and rubbish disposal facilities. Two hefty swing-bridges span the Weaver at Northwich, but both have sufficient headroom to allow most inland waterway craft to pass beneath without requiring them to be swung, though it may be a different matter for the high-masted yachts which migrate upriver for the winter. Between the swing-bridges the navigation widens into a sizeable pool: egress point of the unnavigable

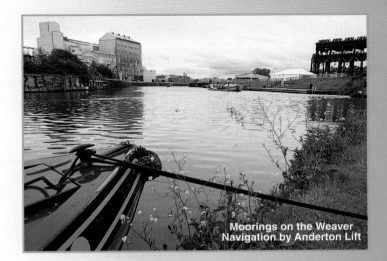

Moorings on the Weaver Navigation by Anderton Lift

Dane; home to a unique floating hotel; and the location of further (and perhaps preferable if you can find space) visitor moorings.

Northwich used to make a living from shipbuilding. Several busy yards were based here turning out narrowboats, wide beam barges, tugs, coasters, river steamers and ferries. Lamentably little remains other than the sites of half a dozen or so yards which existed here in the industry's heyday. Maritime engineering is confined now to British Waterways' maintenance yard with its dainty clock-tower.

HUNTS LOCKS, the first of two upstream of Anderton, are framed by a high railway viaduct carrying the old Cheshire Lines Committee's route from Manchester to Chester. Archive photographs depict Hunts Locks filled with a multiplicity of craft: steam packets, Weaver flats, tugs and launches. What was it the Arabs used to say? Ichabod - the glory has departed. In common with all Weaver locks there are two chambers at Hunts, the smaller being the one now regularly used. Also in evidence

Peaceful moorings on the Weave[r]

are the railway type signals once used to indicate the state of readiness of the locks to approaching shipping.

The lock is hand operated by the lock-keeper. Travelling upstream he'll probably drop you a line in the sense that he'll lower a rope for you to attach your ropes to so as to secure your boat against turbulence as the lock fills. Upstream of Hunts, the channel, by-passing old meanders, is long and relatively straight as far as the Vale Royal railway bridge. This reach is used for rowing and, with footpaths on either bank, is also popular with pedestrians. Fishermen favour this length too, finding it well stocked with good-sized roach, perch, pike, tench and bream. Jalsea Marine's yard usually contains an interesting assortment of craft. Last time we passed these ranged from an American fishing vessel to a torpedo boat! The yard used to belong to Pimblotts who built wide boats for the Leeds & Liverpool Canal, barges for the Bridgewater Department of the MSC, and some of the distinctive steel hulled Admiral class narrowboats.

HARTFORD BRIDGE carries the frenetically busy dual-carriageway Northwich by-pass across the navigation. It is built, uninspiringly but practically, of concrete piers with a steel span. Beyond it the Weaver finally begins to justify its reputation for beauty. Trees spill down to the water's edge, their higher branches framing a lofty sandstone viaduct built by the Grand Junction Railway in 1837 and now carrying the electrified West Coast Main Line across the Weaver Navigation. From these hurrying trains you catch tantalising glimpses of the Weaver luxuriating in its wooded cutting, but by water the journey is so much slower and the sense of intimacy correspondingly deeper. Set on a bend - so that, whichever way you are travelling, they remain out of sight until the last moment - VALE ROYAL LOCKS are amongst the loveliest on the inland waterways. The lock-keeper has one of those jobs you'd kill for. He's something of a bird-watcher, and lists of recent sightings adorn the window of his lockside office.

Downstream

Turn right out of the Anderton Lift, and you'll find yourself heading downstream through the river's most industrial zone. Not that it can hold a candle to its commercial heyday. Twenty years ago British Waterways were energetically promoting Anderton as an inland port, and not without effect, three or four ships a week coming up the Weaver with general cargoes for warehousing here. None of that remains now, and an air of sadness hangs over these deserted quays, graffitied with the names of ships that have docked here in the busier past.

SALTERSFORD LOCK lies within spitting distance of the Trent & Mersey Canal. Ironic, isn't it, that the Weaver, progressively invested in and modernised, should now be so quiet, whereas the old canal up on the hillside, virtually unchanged since its construction in the 18th century, is now hugely busy with boats. It's the automated, large chamber which boaters use at Saltersford now. The lock-keeper operates the lock for you, though he has other duties too, being called away to swing the navigation's big bridges when high-masted vessels are in the offing. A small community - a cluster of simple cottages - has grown up here beside the locks in the most idyllic of surroundings. There are visitor moorings downstream of the lock and this is a desirable spot to linger. Below Saltersford the river retreats once more into rural isolation and you're alone again with your thoughts.

CONNOISSEURS regard the Vale Royal Cut as the prettiest stretch of the Weaver, and their opinion is difficult to refute. Characteristically free of roads, woodlands mask the parallel railway, muffling the sound of its trains. The visitor moorings upstream of Vale Royal Locks must rate as one of the most idyllic on the inland waterways network. In medieval times there was an abbey hereabouts. In subsidence induced flashes, alongside the river, grebes and coots nest on floating lily pads and yellow iris are abundant. Cut your engine if you're boating, and just listen to the birdsong.

New Bridge rarely swings now, inertia has set in from lack of regular use since shipping ceased upstream of Northwich in the Sixties. With a maximum headroom of 6ft 8ins, it's a tight fit, but most pleasure craft can slip through and progress upstream to Winsford.

The bosky charm of Vale Royal gives way to Little Siberia as the Weaver negotiates a reach overlooked by a large rock salt mine, the last one working in the district. Crumbling timber quays recall the river's part in transportation of mid Cheshire salt products. But no longer, and even the Cheshire Lines Committees' branch railway (now converted into a public bridleway) has been abandoned in favour of road transport. Red banks of road salt border the riverbank. The navigation is no longer pretty, but it remains fascinating in a post-industrial sense. And the future will apparently be

greener still, as various land reclamation projects bear fruit. Personally, though, we'd swap them all for a chance encounter with a passing coaster, like all navigations which have lost their trade it is difficult to escape an empty sense of melancholy and lack of purpose.

The town of Winsford gloomily straddles both banks of the Weaver, an industrial abyss dropped in the midst of Cheshire pastures. Colonised by post war Liverpudlian overspill schemes, its economy now seems in the lap of business parks where employees eke out a meagre living. There must have been money here once though, for two railway companies saw fit to build branch lines into the town. The CLC called their station 'Winsford & Over', the LNWR called theirs 'Over & Wharton'. If you were opening a station here now it would have to be called 'Over & Out'.

Winsford Bridges mark the end of British Waterways' jurisdiction of the river, but the local authority indulgently permit gratis exploration of Winsford Bottom Flash, a lake-like expanse of water brought about by subsidence resulting from salt mining. Leaving the river's confines and heading out into the flash is like going out to sea. Gulls enhance this illusion, as do the sailing dinghies. Red buoys mark the shallows, yellow buoys mark the racing zone. Local boaters will tell you that it is possible to drop your anchor and moor midstream, though you may prefer to return to the more orthodox confines of the river. At least you can secretly congratulate yourself you came.

New Bridge
low headroom
6ft 8ins

salt mine

Vale Royal Cut

sluice

Meadowbank

5

Whitegate Way

sewage works

Red Lion

FF

Winsford Bridges
10ft 8ins

Winsford

Winsford (Bottom) Flash

Anderton — Maps 19 & 32

Good moorings, the exciting proximity of 'The Lift' and an adjoining Wildflower Trail render Anderton a favoured stop in many a boating itinerary.

THE MOORINGS - restaurant and coffee shop at Anderton Marina. Tel: 01606 79789.

STANLEY ARMS - canalside opposite Anderton Lift. Food from noon daily. Inn which predates the canal, popular with locals and boaters alike. Bowling green and customer moorings.Tel: 01606 75059.

LIFT CAFETERIA - canalside. Boaters breakfasts available from 9.45am daily at this cafe offering fine views of the Lift. Tel: 01606 786777.

ANDERTON BOAT LIFT - canalside Visitor Centre celebrating the Lift and local canals in all their historic glory. A widebeam trip boat named Edwin Clark after the Lift's designer offers 30 minute trips up or down the Lift. River trips to Northwich and back are also usually available. Tel: 01606 786777.

CANAL EXPLORER - narrowboat trips along the Trent & Mersey Canal. Tel: 01565 750461.

ANDERTON NATURE PARK - waymarked trails through reclaimed wasteland where many plants usually confined to coastal environments thrive in the local salty soils. Tel: 01606 77741

Local buses run to Northwich at regular intervals. Tel: 0870 608 2 608.

Marston — Maps 19

Former salt mining village still wrought by the lopsided scars of the past. Useful general store accessible to west of bridge 192 and pub called the SALT BARGE (Tel: 01606 43064) by Bridge 193. LION SALT WORKS - Bridge 193. Gradually being restored, the site is now open daily, whilst an indoor exhibition and shop is open most afternoons. Tel: 01606 41823.

Wincham Wharf — Map 19

Busy boating centre close to Lostock Gralam railway station. THE WHARF is a warehouse conversion adjoining Bridge 189. Tel: 01606 46099.

Broken Cross — Map 19

Canalside at Bridge 184 stands the OLD BROKEN CROSS refurbished in the modern manner - Tel: 01606 40431. Smithy with canalia opposite. Garage with SPAR shop less than 5 minutes walk to south-east.

Acton Bridge — Maps 18 & 34

Scattered community on hillside overlooking the Trent & Mersey Canal and the River Weaver. Forge and nursery adjacent to Bartington Wharf on the Trent & Mersey Canal. Popular with boaters both on the Trent & Mersey and Weaver on account of the close proximity of a number of pubs.

LEIGH ARMS - Tel: 01606 853327. Comfortable pub overlooking Acton Swing Bridge featuring stained glass windows of commercial river scenes of the past.

THE HORNS - Tel: 01606 852192. Country pub located between the canal and the river offering food and bed & breakfast.

RIVERSIDE INN - Tel: 01606 852310. Riverside inn with customer moorings and waterside patio. Two more nice country pubs up in the village if you care to stretch your legs: THE MAYPOLE (Tel: 01606 853114) and HAZEL PEAR (Tel: 01606 853195). There are no shops within easy reach of either waterway but fairly frequent buses (Tel: 0870 608 2 608) will take you swiftly to Northwich or Warrington. Acton Bridge railway station can be a useful staging point for towpath walkers, but be warned the timetable is sparse. Tel: 08457 484950 for details.

Northwich — Map 32

Surprisingly large, and unexpectedly likeable, you can tell that Northwich is off the beaten track because it still retains a good number of 5 figure telephone numbers. Handy moorings offer instant access to the town's pedestrianised shopping streets characterized by handsome but ersatz half-timber buildings built to combat subsidence.

DE SOUZA'S - High Street. Bustling Italian trattoria. Tel: 01606 43203

FLOATEL - Watling Street by Town Bridge. Floating bar and restaurant. Tel: 01606 44443.

NORTHWICH SEAFARER - Watling Street. Fish & chip restaurant & takeaway. Tel: 01606 43169.

Excellent retail market Tue, Fri & Sat. Locally grown fruit and veg from FIRST CHOICE FRUIT on Leicester Street. Fine butchers called WEBB & SONS on Witton Street. Large branch of M&S on Leicester Street and BRATTS department store in the High Street.

TOURIST INFORMATION - Watling Street. Tel: 01606 353534.

THE SALT MUSEUM - London Road. The story of Cheshire salt making from Roman times to the present day in a museum housed in a former workhouse. Tel: 01606 41331.

DOCK ROAD PUMPING STATION - restored sewage pumping works, sadly only open Sunday afternoons but highly recommended none the less. Tel: 01457 864187.

VALE ROYAL CRUISES - trips along the Weaver aboard a converted Dutch barge. Tel: 01606 40295.

BUSES - useful links with Trent & Mersey at Barnton, Anderton etc; also to/from Winsford and Acton Bridge for walks along the Weaver. Tel: 0870 608 2 608.

TRAINS - local services to/from Chester, Stockport & Manchester from station approx 1 mile east of town centre. Tel: 08457 484950.

34 WEAVER NAVIGATION

Acton Bridge & Dutton 4mls/1lk/1hr

UP on the busy waters of the Trent & Mersey you can count the passing roofs of boats. Down here on the Weaver you sense that you're far from the madding crowd. Dutton Lock and Acton Swing Bridge thus provoke welcome interludes of interest. Tall Lombardy poplar trees seem to be a feature of the riverbank, marking its progress along the valley's pasturelands.

The river splits into two channels at ACTON BRIDGE, where the woman who used to wave pink knickers and a whisky bottle at passing ships, has moved on to a better world filled with angels who are always doing such things. Of the two channels, the northernmost is the main, the southern having been adopted for linear moorings by the local cruising club.

Impressively muscular, Acton Swing Bridge spans both channels, pivoting on a central pontoon. It dates from 1933. Evidence of an earlier bridge lies adjacent, one arch still spanning the smaller, boat-filled channel.

DUTTON LOCK demands a degree of concentration, but compensates with the opportunity to pass the time of day with the resident lock-keeper. Visually it is typical of the river's modernised locks, replete with

redundant semaphore signals and dual chambers. Downstream the old towpath is carried across a backwater upon an elegant timber side bridge, but, as bridges go, it is Joseph Locke's Dutton (or Weaver) Viaduct, built in 1837 for the Grand Junction Railway, that steals the scene. Virgin Pendolinos swan haughtily across it at well over a hundred miles an hour, but for once you know with peculiar clarity where you'd rather be.

The bridge at PICKERING'S WHARF has long gone and the residents of the two houses on the north bank have to cross the river - with their groceries and chattels - by boat. West of here the Weaver goes all shy and retiring, becoming the haunt of otters and cormorants, negotiating a series of luxuriantly wooded reaches which remind one forcibly of the Dart downstream of Totnes.

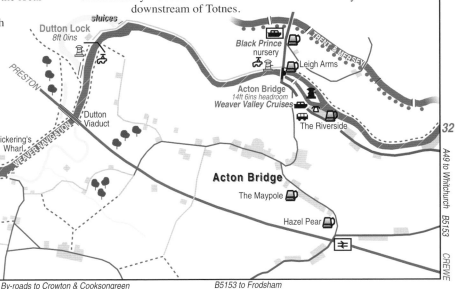

sluices

Dutton Lock
8ft 0ins

Black Prince
nursery

Leigh Arms

Acton Bridge
14ft 6ins headroom
Weaver Valley Cruises

The Riverside

PRESTON

Dutton
Viaduct

Pickering's
Wharf

WEAVER NAVIGATION

TRENT & MERSEY

*Silver
Well*

Crewood Hall

Acton Bridge

The Maypole

Hazel Pear

By-roads to Crowton & Cooksongreen

B5153 to Frodsham

32

A49 to Whitchurch   B5153   CREWE

*I*F it's good scenery you're after, your voyage down the Weaver need progress no further than the entrance to the old Frodsham Cut. Beyond this point the navigation is rapidly sucked into the industrial entrails of Runcorn. Another channel leads, over a weir, to the river's original course. Adjacent to the site of Sutton Lock, submerged in the river's reedy margin, there's an eerie cemetery of wooden barges - Weaver flats and Brunner steamers.

Three bridges span the navigation as it pursues an artificial course to the east of the town of Frodsham. One is a typical Weaver swing bridge, one a lofty railway bridge, and one a modern motorway structure. A vast chemical works dominates the last mile of the Weaver Navigation whilst dredgers pump silt into lagoons on the opposite bank.

Weston Marsh leads down into the Manchester Ship Canal. Without special arrangement, craft licensed with British Waterways cannot proceed any further unless they opt to explore the short Weston Canal leading to the now defunct Weston Point Docks. Sadly, for those who like to cruise in circles, the Runcorn & Weston Canal no longer links with the Bridgewater Canal at Runcorn. Perhaps the last

authenticated journey along this missing link was John Seymour's *Voyage Into England* in the mid Sixties. Though already officially abandoned, he managed to effect a passage, much to the consternation of the authorities who were left with no option other than to run vast quantities of water down from the Bridgewater to facilitate recovery of the Seymours' boat from the closed canal.

As for ourselves, we were not tempted to call the authorities' bluff, though we did push through the undergrowth to where the entrance lock to the Runcorn & Weston resides fairly intact, if undoubtedly unusable. We moored by the immobile swing bridge which puts the kibosh on thoughts of exploring Weston Docks and walked along the dispiritingly empty quays to pay homage to the old Weaver Navigation church but found it locked and apparently disused. A ship moved slowly down the Ship Canal towards Eastham. Across the width of the Mersey the old lighthouse at Hale gleamed in the sunshine. A plane landed at the John Lennon airport as we lunched on Scotch broth and *petits de pain*. This wasn't just the end of a canal journey, this was the end of the world.

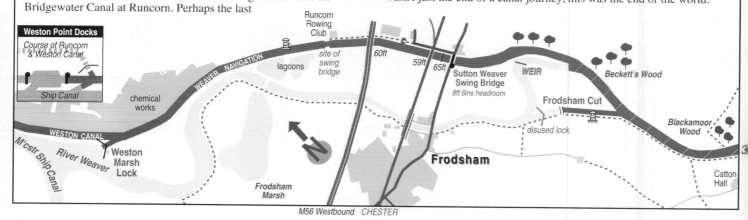

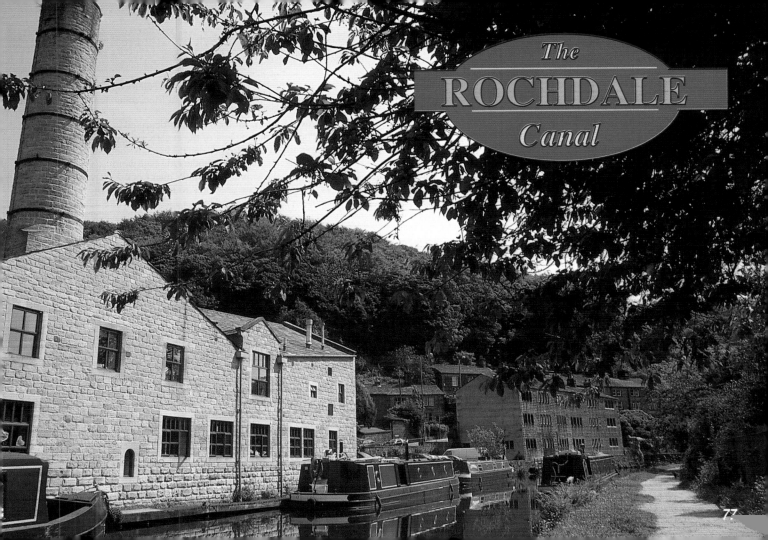

The
ROCHDALE
Canal

*I*T would be naive for us to run away with the idea that the multi-million pound restoration of the Rochdale Canal to full navigability was simply an exercise in catering for the wanderlust of narrow-boaters. Big business (as in most of life) is behind the Rochdale's regeneration, and those of us who enjoy exploring canals by boat are simply the beneficiaries of a commercial by-product. That said, one can only marvel at the astonishing volte-face in the Rochdale Canal's fortunes, and the incredible speed with which it has been returned to navigable status. Twenty-five years ago it was a miracle that one could use the city centre section of the canal in circumnavigating the Cheshire Ring, now the whole route across the Pennines to Yorkshire is available for exploration - only the little matter of ninety-two locks in thirty-two miles can deter the potential boater, though it is mandatory that you book your passage with British Waterways on 01925 847725.

Opened throughout in 1804, the Rochdale Canal leaves Manchester's Dale Street Basin and immediately establishes its character by negotiating a couple of locks in quick succession. Numbered 83 and 82 in the sequence, it should be remembered that locks 84-92 are part of the

Cheshire Ring described on Map 11. Between locks 82 and 81 the canal is overlooked by some fine examples of Mancunian textile mills, many of which are being refurbished as flats.

Weaving through a hitherto socially-deprived area which will hopefully be another recipient of the canal's ability to regenerate both bricks and mortar and people's lives, the canal is soon encountering more locks, from which there is little respite until Failsworth is reached. Another fine example of mill architecture broods over Lock 79. The reach between locks 77 and 76 has been deepened to make adjustments for mining subsidence.

More housing borders the canal as it makes its way through Newton Heath where handy local shops (and a busy market on Mondays, Wednesdays and Saturdays) are within easy reach of Lock 69. Newton Heath was the original home of one of the world's most famous football clubs - Manchester United! - who developed from a railway workers amateur team. Canalside street names such as Silk and Millwright echo a lost era of textile activity, though several of the mills live on. By Lock 67 Failsworth Home Guard manfully still anticipate an invasion which fortunately for us never materialised..

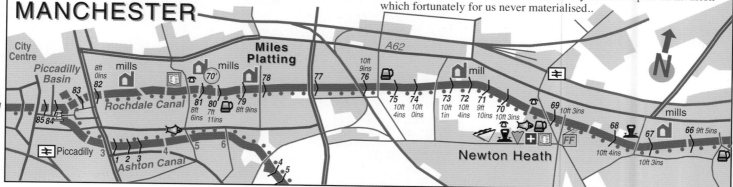

*Figures relate to Rochdale Canal east of Piccadilly Basin

A WELCOME breather between locks manifests itself in the vicinity of Failsworth. Time to pay attention to the surrounding scenery perhaps. The Rochdale Canal's commercial zenith was shortlived on account of the onset of the Railway Age, but at least its wide beam barges provided capacious logistical resource for a multitude of waterside mills and sundry other industries which rapidly sprang up along the route of the canal. Post-industrially a goodly number of factories have vanished, but many mills stubbornly remain, many converted to new uses, but some still engaged in the textile trade. Ivy Mill, by Lock 65, was appropriated for the manufacture of munitions during the Second World War.

Failsworth is particularly rich in fine examples of mill architecture, to which the re-born canal lends fresh perspective. On the opening day in 1804 - when heavy frosts threatened to put a damper on celebrations by freezing the canal entirely - the band of the First Battalion of Manchester & Salford Independent Volunteers boarded one of the first vessels to pass along the canal and enlivened its passage by regaling bystanders with popular tunes of the day.

Between Failsworth and the M60 the canal passes under the railway line to Oldham and traverses a green corridor, an unlikely oasis much favoured by fishermen of all ages and, surprisingly, both sexes. Wriggling through a cats cradle of motorways and dual-carriageways, the canal enters an uninspiring zone of wastegrounds and modern warehouses, one bearing the good old canal associated name of Widdop. When the motorway was built, supporters of restoration of the Rochdale Canal managed to win a landmark battle in Parliament to have a culvert of navigable dimensions included in the scheme so as to safeguard the canal's future. Some sources recommend the Boat & Horses pub (by the A663 road crossing) as a suitable place for overnight mooring, others would have you press on to the more countrified Rose of Lancaster at Chadderton on Map 38.

Oldham's skyline of chimneys, spires and high-rises rears up to the east but doesn't necessarily inspire a desire for closer acquaintance. Middleton Junction no longer lives up to its railway origins, the branch lines to Oldham and Middleton having been Beechinged out of existence, but it remains the location of the Greengate Brewery of J. W. Lees & Co, family brewers in the vicinity since 1828. Grimshaw Lane Lift Bridge is operated electrically and lifts (unusually) on a horizontal plane. It is overlooked by the massive Swan Mill, an outlier of many still extant in Oldham. It was erected for the Swan Cotton Spinning Company in 1875 and continued in production until 1959, notwithstanding a serious fire in 1922. These days it provides commodious premises for a manufacturer of furniture foam, and the workforce, sans clogs sans shawls, all seem sadly to arrive for their shifts by car.

Map labels:
- 38
- Grimshaw Lane Lift Bridge
- Middleton Junction
- Swan Mill
- B6189
- 70' Oldham Broadway Bridge
- Travelodge
- A663 mills
- Boat & Horses
- M60
- A6104
- Moston rly sta
- Morrisons
- B6393
- A663
- New Moston
- mill
- 9ft 9ins
- 65
- Failsworth
- 70'
- 36

BY Rochdale Canal standards, Lock 64 is oddly isolated. Eastbound it precedes another traditionally built up area of mills and housing on the road between Middleton and Oldham. There's a convivial pub called the Rose of Lancaster beside the canal at this point serving locally brewed Lees beers as well as an Indian take-away. Vinegary aromas issue from Sarsons' works near Mills Hill railway station.

An idyllic passage follows as the canal twists to cross a headwater of the River Irk before commencing the ascent through two lock flights. The railway (Manchester to Bradford) thrusts its more confident way across the valley on a hefty embankment: more demurely the canal follows the contours before accepting that there's nothing for it but to gird its loins and climb. Formerly four track, the railway has been reduced to two, suffering almost the same fate as the canal in terms of freight carried - nowadays the M62 bears the brunt of Trans Pennine goods. The original double track railway bridge is of particularly handsome design.

Slattocks is said to be a corruption of 'South Locks'. The top lock, No.54, heralds a welcome mile long pound. Overnight mooring is recommended here with a pub - the Hopwood Arms - on hand and an enterprising Post Office (Tel: 0161 643 2359) doubling as THE VILLAGE PANTRY offering 'freshly made, quality sandwiches' Monday to Friday 9am-2pm.

One of the biggest challenges facing the engineers involved in re-opening the Rochdale Canal was to pass under the M62 motorway. Fortunately, a culvert for a farm track provided a possible answer. Thus a deviation from the canal's original course has been essayed at significantly less cost than once anticipated. At the same time, Lock 53 has been re-sited to the south of the motorway. The 'floating towpath' provided to pass walkers beneath the motorway doesn't seem to be in regular use, and they currently face a dispiriting detour via the A664.

The motorway did, however, irrevocably eliminate the canal's Heywood Branch, though perhaps at some point in the future it might be re-dug on a new course to provide access to the East Lancashire preserved steam railway which runs between Heywood, Bury and Rawtenstall. The East Lancs locomotives occasionally escape from captivity to haul an excursion on the main line, and you may see one steaming off the curve past the track maintenance depot at Castleton.

After the rural interlude of Slattocks, the Rochdale Canal is reintroduced to industrialisation at Castleton. One mill has found new life as a water activity centre, others are more inscrutable as to their purpose, but gone is Tweedale & Smalley's once massive textile machinery factory, the Globe Works.

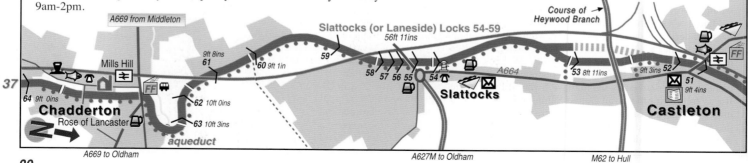

MUCH as the Macclesfield Canal snubs its home town, so the Rochdale passes a goodly distance to the east of its namesake. On this occasion, however, a branch canal was constructed to bear the brunt of local goods. Its course is still apparent, albeit derelict. Yet who knows, it may one day be revived as part of the regeneration of east Rochdale promised with the (much delayed!) extension to the town of Manchester's Metrolink tram system.

Rochdale lies down in a valley, and so it made sense for the canal builders to avoid going too close to the town. Clinging to the contours, they managed to avoid heavy lockage, and as a result there are only two locks on the whole of this map, a blessed relief, though there are - by way of variety - two swing bridges to contend with.

The canal restorationists were faced with a major road blockage at Edinburgh Way. Resourceful engineering, and a determination previously unknown in the inland waterways' confrontation with road developments, won the day, though at the expense of the

towpath user who is again faced with a detour.

Moss Locks are couched in a typical urbanscape of textile mills - once there were no less than fifteen cotton mills alongside the canal. Between the locks a small branch dog-legged off the main line to serve yet more cotton mills, its egress still apparent. Oldham Road once bore the tracks of the grandiosely named Manchester, Bury, Rochdale & Oldham Steam Tramway. The last electric tram ran in Rochdale in 1931, but, of course, one trusts, implicity, that they are coming back once central government has sorted out its priorities.

The Pennine hills, which have been shadowing your progress out of Manchester like Red Indians keeping tabs on a wagon train, begin to let themselves be seen: intimidatingly, you have to cross them! A forgotten little farmhouse stands balefully beside the first swingbridge, beyond it a typically Pennine view opens out framed by a swarthy railway embankment. Beyond Firgrove Bridge the Rochdale Canal finally shakes off urbanisation. Paralleling the railway which captured so much of its trade, the canal passes through a shallow shale cutting before reaching Clegg Hall and a boarded up old mill of stone construction. Smithy Bridge railway station is handily canalside for towpath walkers.

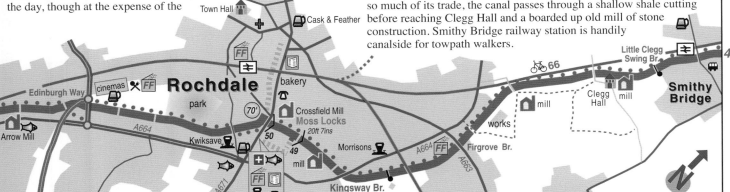

Rather less than prepossessing from the canal, Rochdale repays those persistent enough to make the fifteen minute walk in from the canal by Lock 50. The Town Hall is simply astonishing (guided tours at 2.15pm on Fridays) and would do justice to many a grander town.

CASK & FEATHER - Oldham Road (10 minutes walk from Lock 50) Tel: 01702 711746. CAMRA recommended home brew pub. LA MANCHA - The Butts. Town centre Spanish restaurant. Tel: 01706 713400.
If you enjoy Indian food, make your way to Milkstone Road (just north of the railway station) where you'll come upon an array of ethnic restaurants and takeaways.

The Exchange and Wheatsheaf shopping malls host all the usual high street names. More lively and authentic is the traditional covered market, open daily save for Sundays. Local shops handy for the canal are marked on the map.

(i) TOUCHSTONES/TIC - The Esplanade. Tel: 01706 864928. Refurbished art gallery, TIC and bookshop (including a small secondhand section stocked by Kelsalls of Littleborough), the gallery features the work of Frederick William Jackson who was born at Middleton Junction in 1859, and who became one of the 'Staithes Group' based on the North Yorkshire coast at the end of the 19th century.
PIONEERS MUSEUM - Toad Lane. Tel: 0161 832 4300. Celebration of the Rochdale Pioneers who founded the Co-operative movement in 1844. *Not open on Mondays.*

TRAINS - links along the Calder Valley and to/from Oldham and Manchester. Tel: 08457 484950.
TAXIS - Streamline. Tel: 01706 644104.

A traveller in the days before the canal or railway came to Littleborough, found it "a very desirable retreat when it is found impossible to ascend the mountains, during the continuance of the howling storm." Nothing much has changed, for there is still an inclination to sit tight in Littleborough, waiting for the skies to clear before tackling the summit.

THE WATERSIDE INN - canalside. Food and accommodation. Tel: 01706 376250.
THE SUMMIT - cosy pub adjacent to western end of canal summit. Thwaites beer, bar & restaurant meals. Tel: 01706 378011.

Surprisingly extensive facilities including: Co-op supermarket adjacent to railway station. Nat West, Barclays and Yorkshire banks. Kelsall's antiquarian bookshop is excellent. Launderette on Victoria Street.

(i) COACH HOUSE HERITAGE CENTRE - Tel: 01706 378481. Closed Mondays. Exhibitions of Littleborough's history and tearooms. Also Tourist Information.

TRAINS - half-hourly Calder Valley link with Todmorden and Rochdale; (hourly with Walsden). Tel: 08457 484950.

Coneygreen Lock No.62

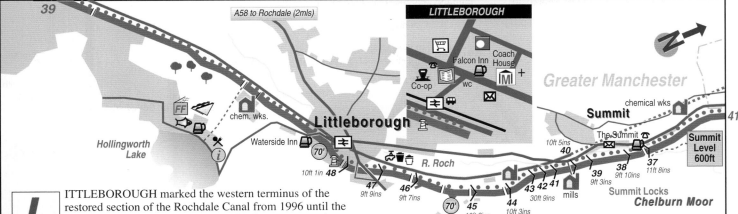

LITTLEBOROUGH

Falcon Inn · Coach House · Co-op · wc

Greater Manchester

chemical wks

Summit

Summit Level 600ft

The Summit

Hollingworth Lake

chem. wks.

Littleborough

Waterside Inn

A58 to Rochdale (2mls)

70' · 10ft 1in **48**

47 9ft 9ins · **46** 9ft 7ins · R. Roch · 70' · **45** 10ft 3ins · **44** 10ft 3ins · **43** · **42** · **41** 30ft 9ins · mills

10ft 5ins · **40** · **39** 9ft 3ins · **38** 9ft 10ins · **37** 11ft 8ins

Summit Locks
Chelburn Moor

LITTLEBOROUGH marked the western terminus of the restored section of the Rochdale Canal from 1996 until the complete re-opening of 2002. Now it's just a punctuation mark on the complete canal, though with a dozen locks to be tackled to the east, it continues to be a popular mooring point in either direction: westbound travellers tumbling down into Littleborough with relief; eastbound summoning up the nerve to tackle yet another closely spaced flight of locks, through which passage must again be booked with British Waterways (Tel: 01925 847725) to ensure the best use of precious water supplies.

The outskirts of Littleborough turn a somewhat blank face as the canal skirts its eastern periphery, but it's a welcoming little town where solace can be found along the shelves of Kelsall's excellent secondhand bookshop, or, if literature is not your bent, by simply watching your underwear go round and round in the launderette. If it's fun you want, make your way to Hollingworth Lake, a canal reservoir disguised as a seaside resort for Rochdale folk who lack the means or the misplaced energy to make it to Blackpool.

With the little River Roch in tow, the Rochdale Canal gets quickly 'stuck in', as a series of locks carry it up past the old Rock Nook cotton mills. One or two of the locks have distorted walls which prevent two narrowboats sharing them side by side. Did you notice how the Roch is taken over the railway by the western portal of Summit Tunnel in an iron trough?

By Benthouse Lock a slender, angled dock complete with stump of crane hints at former commerce. Although shown on the 1911, 6in OS map, no corresponding works caught our eye. Perhaps there was some intercourse with Stephenson's new fangled railway, or with the quarry at nearby Windy Bank. Several mills have disappeared. Durn Mill dealt, unusually for Lancashire, in woollens.

A quiet sense of pride and achievement marks your attainment of the summit, 600 feet above sea level. The Hills of the North rejoice around your shoulders. Enjoy your brief sense of hubris, the summit pound is less than a mile long!

41 ROCHDALE CANAL

Todmorden 5mls/22lks/6hrs

THE late eighteenth century navvies could hardly have faced a wilder landscape in which to construct a man-made waterway than the Rochdale Canal's route over its boggy morass of a summit; the watershed between the catchment areas of the Mersey to the west, and the Ouse to the east. Southern hills may roll politely - Pennine hills flagellate themselves into a frenzy of millstone grit revivalism. Coming down from the summit it is difficult not to feel like Moses returning from the mountain. The locals regard you expectantly, as if you might be carrying news of additional commandments such as: 'Thou shall make sure all gates are closed when leaving a lock'; 'Thou shall not leave paddles raised'; and 'Thou shall not cast covetous glances upon the public house until six pm'.

Locks with lovely names like Winterbutlee and Nip Square lower the canal out of the hills into a land of textile mills. The short intervening pounds have a tendency to spill over into reedy margins. Walsden and Gauxholme sound like a pair of hefty, battle-hardened centre backs who might have played for Burnley after the war. In reality Gauxholme boasts one of the great canalscapes in the kingdom, its most potent image the canal's passage beneath the Gothically inspired, cast iron railway bridge with battlemented abutments, particularly photogenic from the neighbouring hillside.

The 'Great Wall of Todmorden' (a massive blue brick retaining wall supporting the adjoining railway's former goods yard) precedes the town itself, a glorious northern community couched under Stoodley Pike, a monument which sits like a rocket about to be launched on the moors.

40
Longlees Lock
12ft 0ins
35 10ft 10ins
34 10ft 1in
36
Bird i' th' Hand
Summit Tunnel
33
11ft 0ins
32 9ft 3ins
Deanroyd Bridge
31
9ft 6ins
30 11ft 0ins
10ft 2ins
29
28 9ft 2ins
10ft 3ins
27
Hollins Mill
Walsden
West Yorks
Walsden Moor
26
9ft 1ins
25
10ft 5ins
Gauxholme
former warehouse
24
23
22
Gauxholme Locks
30ft 2ins
viaduct
21
20 10ft 2ins
Dobroyd Castle
Centre Vale Park
Todmorden
Morrisons
Todmorden (Library) Lock
19
10ft 7ins
WALSDEN
8ft 9ins 18
Co-op
Baltimore Marina
9ft 3ins 17
Woodhouse Mill Bridge
Woodhouse Mill
old quarry
10ft 6ins 16
Rose & Crown
Castle Street
viaduct
Picnic Site & Hillside Walks
Pickwell & Arnold
9ft 5ins 15
dyeworks
42
A646 to Hebden Bridge
TODMORDEN
Library
Rochdale Road
Water St
Dale St
Halifax Road
TH
market
wc
70'

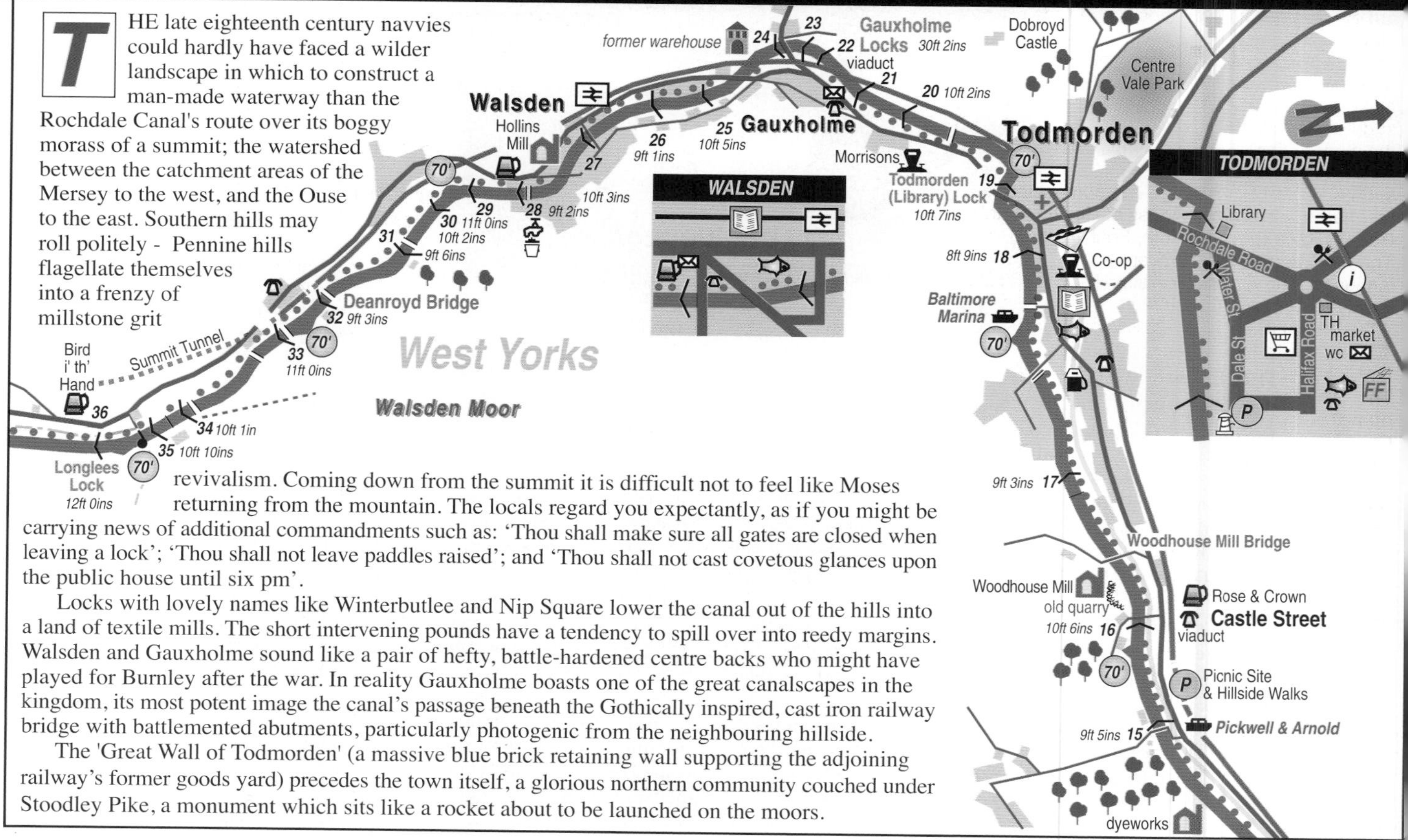

Walsden
Map 41

Walsden snuggles cosily in its steep sided valley out of the worst that the moorland winds would otherwise throw at it. It's a mid Pennine community in microcosm, with textile mills and dyeworks (and a strange occupation called 'picker' making) taking advantage of the fast-flowing water supply, and with the scars of former quarrying on the slopes. They even dug coal from primitive shafts up on the tops, where the miners rubbed shoulders with hill farmers. The nomenclature resonates with the harshness of life: Top o' th' Rough, Rake End, Jail Hole, Foul Clough Road, Thorns Greece and Pot Oven. It's like another language. And perhaps it was, after all, 'Walsden' is said to derive from "Valley of the Welshmen."

VILLAGE CHIPPY - adjacent Hollings Lock. Brilliant fish & chip shop in the same Pollard family for 90 years. Featuring home made pies. They work so hard during the week that they don't open Saturday or Sunday. Tel: 01706 815769.

CROSS KEYS INN - adjacent Lock 28. Tel: 01706 815185. Bar and restaurant meals available at this cosy pub which backs on to the canal.

Newsagents adjacent to Hollings Lock. Post office adjacent Travis Mill Lock.

TRAINS - hourly, daily services linking Walsden with useful towpath-walking stages at Littleborough and Rochdale to the south and Todmorden and Hebden Bridge to the north. Tel: 08457 484950.

Todmorden
Map 41

Nineteenth century Todmorden lay half in Lancashire, half in Yorkshire. The Town Hall - "classical, yet with a certain crisp and sensuous elegance" according to Pevsner - topped by sculpted figures representing the commerce of each county, straddled the boundary. It is typical

of the town's rich roll call of fine Victorian buildings enhanced by its setting between the steep bifurcating valleys of the Calder and its tributary, Walsden Water. Local hero, John Fielden, is remembered by a statue in Centre Vale Park,

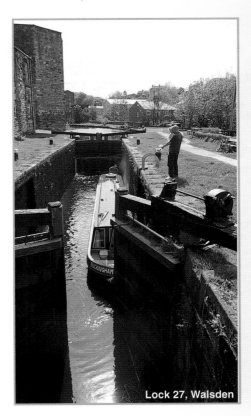
Lock 27, Walsden

recalling that he was largely responsible for the Ten Hours Act of 1847, a landmark in industrial reforms preventing employees from working more than a ten hour day which seems to have been conveniently forgotten. 'Tod's' latest claim to fame is that it was used in the filming of Pawel Pawlikowski's 2004 film *My Summer of Love*. Asked why he chose Todmorden, the young Polish director's reply was perhaps lost in translation: "I am interested in the forgotten places, the dumping grounds."

THE BEAR - Rochdale Road (adjacent Library Lock). Vegetarian cafe located on first floor of former premises of Todmorden Industrial Co-operative store. Open daily. Wonderfully informal atmosphere complete with an unobtrusive children's play area and a comfortable sofa surrounded by vigorous potted plants where you can recover from the arduous Rochdale with cheese and spinach flan and iced grapefruit blush. Tel: 01706 819690.

SINCLAIRS - White Hart Fold. Cafe/bistro. Tel: 01706 817828.

ROSE & CROWN - on main road near Woodhouse Mill Bridge. Quaint stone pub offering good food, quiet and Taylor's Landlord. Tel: 01706 812428.

THE VEDAS - Rochdale Road. Tel: 01706 814009. Sophisticated Indian restaurant.

Wonderful indoor market (Mon-Sat, early closing Tue); Morrisons and Co-op supermarkets. Look out for THE BEAR'S ground floor wholefood shop.

(i) TOURIST INFORMATION - Burnley Road. Tel: 01706 818181.

TRAINS - half-hourly connections with Manchester (via Rochdale) and Leeds (via Halifax). Tel: 08457 484950. BUSES to/from Burnley. Tel: 0870 608 2 608.

TAXIS - JB. Tel: 01706 814494.

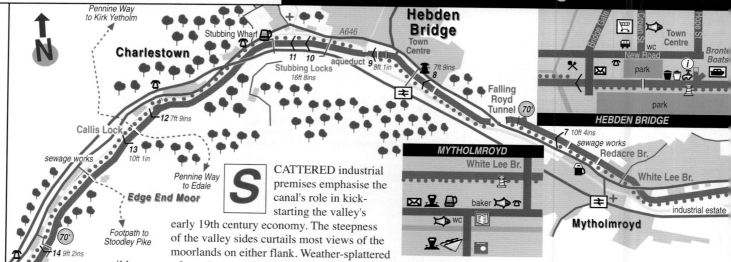

Pennine Way to Kirk Yetholm

N

Charlestown

Stubbing Wharf

Hebden Bridge

Town Centre

A646

11 10 aqueduct 9 8ft 1in

Stubbing Locks
16ft 8ins

8 7ft 9ins

12 7ft 9ins

Callis Lock

13 10ft 1in

sewage works

Pennine Way to Edale

Edge End Moor

Footpath to Stoodley Pike

70'

14 9ft 2ins

41

Falling Royd Tunnel

70'

7 10ft 4ins
sewage works

Redacre Br.

White Lee Br.

industrial estate

Mytholmroyd

MYTHOLMROYD

White Lee Br.

baker

wc

Town Centre

wc

New Road

park

HEBDEN BRIDGE

park

Bridge Gate · Crown St · Hope St

Bronte Boats

SCATTERED industrial premises emphasise the canal's role in kick-starting the valley's early 19th century economy. The steepness of the valley sides curtails most views of the moorlands on either flank. Weather-splattered wilderness of peat bogs and moss are up there unseen, shadowing your progress along the valley's gutter-like floor, but abseiling down to cross the canal by Callis Lock, the Pennine Way rubber-stamps its seal of approval on your journey. Many long distance back-packers, needing the reassurance of civilisation in the midst of all these Pennine wastes, make a detour into Hebden Bridge as did John Hillaby in his *Journey Through Britain* first published in 1968, the lyrical description of a walk from Land's End to John O' Groats. A Yorkshireman anyway, Hillaby felt at home in Hebden, a town where conversation was kept tersely to its essentials - these days they seem much more talkative, the mellowing influence of tourism no doubt. Freshly stone-blasted buildings reflect the gentrification of Hebden and passing boaters are apt to become the cynosure of many a gongoozling eye.

Burnley Road, the A646, provides a busy counterpart to the canal. During the first third of the 20th Century an electric tramway followed its course. Nowadays, M62 notwithstanding, it hosts an almost constant stream of heavy Trans Pennine traffic. The Rochdale Canal is a much quieter alternative. Too quiet in some respects, for it frustratingly doesn't seem to have attracted the number of boats which restoration deserved, a regrettable state of affairs given the splendour of the scenery and the charming character of Calderdale's towns and villages. The locks are challenging, to be sure, but on a grander, more epic scale to the narrow canals of the midlands and south.

Hebden can lay claim to movie fame of a much longer pedigree than Todmorden up the road. *A Boy, A Girl And A Bike* was filmed here in 1949 and starred Honor Blackman, Diana Dors and Anthony Newley. More topically, Hebden recently earned the cachet of Britain's most unique shopping town, a fact which emphasises that its economy no longer relies on the manufacture of fustian (a sort of thick, twilled cloth) but on attracting tourists. There are even New Age overtones which make it appear, at times, like a northern version of Totnes. But in its setting, deep within the wooded folds of the Calder gorge, and in its sturdy, honey-coloured stone buildings, it transcends any tendency to quaintness, whilst there are many fascinating nooks and crannies waiting to be discovered by the diligent explorer. The poetess, Sylvia Plath, is buried at nearby Heptonstall, a picturesque former weaving village just a short (if steep) walk away.

RIM NAM - canalside. Tel: 01422 846888. Thai restaurant overlooking canal basin.
ORGANIC HOUSE - Market Street. Tel: 01422 843429.
THE RUNCIBLE SPOON - Market Street. Tel: 01422 845524. Stylish coffee shop & bistro.
THEO'S - Bridge Gate. Tel: 01422 845337. Lively Greek restaurant (without a licence, so bring your own wine).
IL MULINO - St Georges Square. Italian based in ivy-clad, chimney-topped mill. Tel: 01422 844181.
CROWN FISHERIES - Crown Street. Excellent fish & chip restaurant or takeaway. Tel: 01422 842599.
STUBBING WHARF - canalside above Stubbing Locks. Cosy pub offering a wide choice of food. Tel: 01422 844107.

The individuality of Hebden's shops is one of its strong-points. Not a supermarket in sight, but an engaging alternative in THE OASIS open 8.30am to 10.30pm 365 days a year! Look out also for WOODEAD'S prize-winning butcher's shop on St George's Square and HOLT'S fruit & fish shop on the corner of New Road and Bridge Gate, and the interesting GREEN SHOP, canalside at Hebble End. Natwest, Yorkshire, Barclays and Lloyds TSB banks, small market on Thursdays, Farmers Market first Sunday in the month. Sadly, HATCHARD & DAUGHTERS hitherto excellent antiquarian bookshop was up for sale when we last passed, there is, however, a good new bookshop called BOOKCASE also on Market Street.

i TOURIST INFORMATION - New Road. Tel: 01422 843831. Canalside information centre with permanent exhibition devoted to canals.
PICTURE HOUSE - New Road. Tel: 01422 842807. Classic cinema with interesting programmes of off-beat films.
BRONTE BOATS - canal trips aboard the wide-beam vessel *Verdopolis*. Tel: 01422 845557.
BORDER HERITAGE - Tel: 01706 876893. Heritage bus service (using ex LT 'Routemaster') linking HB with Rawtenstall (for the East Lancs Railway) and Keighley (for the Keighley & Worth Valley). Also stops at Bacup, Todmorden and Haworth. Summer season only on Tue, Wed, Sat, Sun & Bank Hols.

TRAINS - frequent Calder Valley service connecting with Sowerby Bridge and Todmorden, good for towpath walks. Tel: 08457 484950 or 0113 245 7676. Nice old-fashioned Lancashire & Yorkshire station with coffee shop.
CYCLE HIRE - Blazing Saddles on Market Street. Tel: 01422 844435.

Cobbett is said to have slanderously likened Mytholmroyd to the wastes of Nova Scotia. Certainly, around the same time, gangs of lawless 'coiners' operated counterfeit mints in the district. By the time the industrial revolution had kicked-in, however, the village could boast seven cotton mills. Nowadays it is perhaps best known as the birthplace of the poet Ted Hughes (who caught his first pike in the Rochdale Canal in the 1930s) Mytholmroyd is a typical Calder Valley village, though in place of the textile industry which once supported it, it is now a centre for the manufacture of furniture. A plaque commemorates Hughes's old home on Aspinall Street where he lived between 1927 and 1938, but there are hopes, locally, that the old station building (unusually higher than it is wide) might be developed into a visitor centre celebrating the poet's life and times.

The village boasts two excellent fish & chip shops (or 'fisheries' now that we are in Yorkshire), BRIDGE END (Tel: 01422 882217) at the west end and BANNISTERS (Tel: 01422 884670) at the east. Overlooking the river bridge, RIVERSIDE CAFE (Tel: 01422 881197) also provides takeaways. The WHITE LION (Tel: 01422 883131) stands canalside by White Lee Bridge and does food except for Tuesday evenings.

JACKSON'S 7-11 store on Burnley Road is complemented by a baker's shop and COWLINGS greengrocery and delicatessen, the latter being located over the river bridge towards the railway station where, tucked down a side street, you'll also find a launderette.

i WALKLEY CLOGS - Midgeley Road. Clog-making mill with shop. Tel: 01422 885757.
TRAINS - as Hebden Bridge. Tel: 08457 484950.

Luddenden Foot   Map 43

Useful sources of sustenance for canallers.
GROVE INN - adjacent Brearley Locks. Food and accommodation. Tel: 01422 883235.
WEAVERS ARMS - Burnley Road. Tel: 01422 882241. Friendly little Thwaites local said to have been frequented (literally) by Branwell Bronte.
OLE SOLE MILO - Burnley Road. Tel: 01422 884102. Italian restaurant in former pub.
MANNY'S - Asian restaurant above canalside pub. Tel: 01422 886640.
ASRAR'S SPICE HOUSE - Burnley Road. Tel: 01422 885835. Fast food outlet.

Sowerby Bridge   Map 43

Sowerby Bridge reminded us, flippantly - not to say irrationally - of Domodossola in the Italian Alps. Perhaps it was the boulder-strewn riverbed; or an empathetic similarity in the high buildings of indigenous stone, stacked precariously upon each other as if on the shelves of an untidy warehouse; or that same, slightly lugubrious sense of a workaday town hewn from a mountain fastness. But when we tried our hesitant Italian on the check-out girl at Kwik Save we got no response; though do you ever?
JAVA RESTAURANT - Wharf Street (opposite canal basin). Indonesian cooking. Tel: 01422 831654.
TEMUJIN - canal basin. Mongolian cooking. Tel: 01422 835500.
GIMBALS - Wharf Street. Fine dining. Tel: 01422 839329.
THE MOORINGS - warehouse conversion at the canal basin. Tel: 01422 833940.
KWIKSAVE & LIDL handy by Deep Lock. Lloyds TSB, Barclays and Yorkshire banks. Market on Tue, Fri & Sat across the river beyond the railway bridge.
TRAINS - Calder Valley services from station easily reached by footpath and alleyway adjacent to fish & chip shop in Wharf Street. Tel: 08457 484950 or 0113 245 7676.

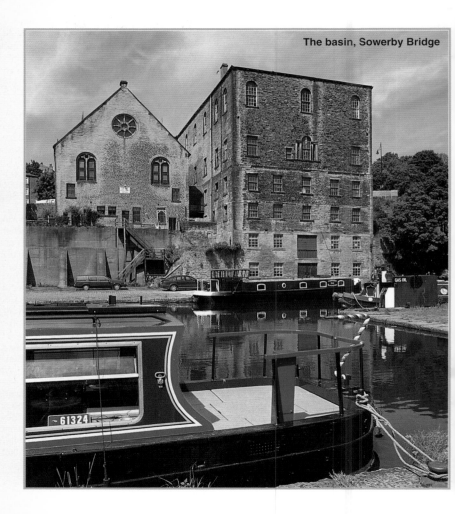

The basin, Sowerby Bridge

PLAYING fields border the canal on the outskirts of MYTHOLMROYD - not least a charming little cricket ground - as the Calder slips unnoticed behind an estate of industrial units. Its name means 'river of stones or hard water', and it makes a journey of over fifty miles from its source above Todmorden to its confluence with the Aire at Castleford.

A good deal of the charm of a boating trip along the heavily-locked Rochdale Canal, lies with the opportunity, every now and then, for you to moor and rest your paddle-gear-weary muscles and walk up on to the neighbouring ridges. Up there the world - or at least this part of the mid-Pennines - is your oyster, and the views can be intoxicating.

To the south of the canal your gaze falls upon Brearley Baptist Chapel and its adjoining Manse. The chapel dates from 1875 and echoes the former role that religion played in alleviating the dull routine of mill work. At the river end of Brearley Lane an end terrace property is known as Little Faith, the locality's original Bethel Chapel.

Brearley Locks lie in an attractive setting overlooked

by woods and adjacent to an ancient stone bridge spanning the Calder. The lower lock is called Edward Kilner after one of the company's engineers. Rochdale locks were 'standardised', as far as feasible, at between nine and ten feet rise so as to simplify the construction of gates and permit them to be interchangeable.

Branwell Bronte, the literary sisters' n'er-do-well brother, was briefly station clerk at LUDDENDEN FOOT, and must have been familiar with, if hardly a habitue of, the gaunt, clock-towered United Reform Church overlooking the canal by Cooper House Mills, and with barges loading at the handsome, four-storey stone warehouse overlooking Boys Park. The past may well, as L.P. Hartley put it, be a 'foreign country', but there are cheap package tours departing daily if you have the imagination to join them. SOWERBY BRIDGE will certainly capture that imagination. The meeting place of the Rochdale and Calder & Hebble canals is full of character and fascinating detail. Moreover, you can modestly rest on your laurels, repairing to the nearest watering-hole with daring tales of your epic Trans Pennine voyage.

Brearley
Grove Inn Brearley Locks
20ft 10ins
70'
6   5
playing
fields
old quarries
Hathershelf Scout

SOWERBY BRIDGE
Shire
Cruisers
Java Temujin
Tunnel
Tuel Lane
Gimbals
Wharf Street
Town
Centre
River Calder
70'

Boys Mill
Luddenden
Foot
Cooper House Mills
Longbottom
Bridge
High Royd
Bridge
sewage
wks.
playing
fields
3/4   2 1
market
Sowerby Bridge Locks 38ft 6ins
Sowerby
Bridge
Calder & Hebble
to Wakefield
BRADFORD
N

Hire Bases

ALVECHURCH BOAT CENTRES - Anderton, Trent & Mersey Canal, Map 19. Tel: 0121 445 2909 *www.alvechurch.com*

ANDERSEN BOATS - Middlewich, Trent & Mersey Canal, Map 21. Tel: 01606 833668 *www.andersenboats.com*

ANGLO-WELSH - New Mills, Peak Forest Canal, Map 7A. Tel: 0117 304 1122 *www.anglowelsh.co.uk*

BLACK PRINCE NARROWBOATS - Bartington, Trent & Mersey Canal, Map 18. Tel: 01527 575115 *www.black-prince.com*

BOLLINGTON WHARF* - Bollington, Macclesfield Canal, Map 5. Tel: 01625 575811.

BRAIDBAR BOAT SERVICES - Higher Poynton, Macclesfield Canal, Map 6. Tel: 01625 873471 *www.braidbarboats.co.uk*

BRIDGEWATER MARINA - Boothstown Basin, Bridgewater Canal, Map 24. Tel: 0161 702 8622.

BRONTE BOATS - Hebden Bridge, Rochdale Canal, Map 42. Tel: 01422 845557 *www.bronteboats.co.uk*

CLAYMOORE NAVIGATION - Preston Brook, Bridgewater Canal, Map 17. Tel: 01928 717273 *www.claymoore.co.uk*

FETTLERS WHARF* - Rufford Arm, Map 30. Tel: 01704 822888.

HERITAGE NARROWBOATS - Scholar Green, Macclesfield Canal, Map 1. Tel: 01782 785700 *www.sherbornewharf.co.uk*

LYMM MARINA* - Lymm, Bridgewater Canal, Map 14. Tel: 01925 752222.

MIDDLEWICH NARROWBOATS - Middlewich, Trent & Mersey Canal, Map 21. Tel: 01606 832460 *www.middlewichboats.co.uk*

PEAK FOREST CRUISERS - Macclesfield, Macclesfield Canal, Map 4. Tel: 01625 424172.

SHIRE CRUISERS - Rochdale Canal, Map 43. Tel: 01422 832712 *www.shirecruisers.co.uk*

THORN MARINE - Stockton Heath, Bridgewater Canal, Map 16. Tel: 01925 265129 *www.thornmarine.co.uk*

* Denotes day boat hire only.

Bridgewater crane near Moore

Boatyards

BALTIMORE MARINA - Todmorden, Rochdale Canal, Map 41. Tel: 01706 818973.
BOLLINGTON WHARF - Bollington, Macclesfield Canal, Map 5. Tel: 01625 575811.
BLACK PRINCE - Bartington Wharf, Trent & Mersey Canal, Map 18. Tel: 01606 852945.
BRAIDBAR BOAT SERVICES - Higher Poynton, Macclesfield Canal, Map 6. Tel: 01625 873471.
EDGE LANE BOATYARD - Stretford, Bridgewater Canal, Map 12. Tel: 0161 864 1066.
EGERTON BOATS - Potato Wharf, Manchester, Bridgewater Canal, Map 11. Tel: 0161 864 1066.
FETTLERS WHARF MARINA - Rufford, Leeds & Liverpool Canal, Map 30. Tel: 01704 822888.
FURNESS VALE MARINA - Furness Vale, Peak Forest Canal, Map 7A. Tel: 01663 742971.
HESFORD MARINE - Lymm, Bridgewater Canal, Map 14. Tel: 01925 754639.
KERRIDGE DRYDOCK - Kerridge, Macclesfield Canal, Map 5. Tel: 01625 574287.
KINGS LOCK BOATYARD - Middlewich, Trent & Mersey Canal, Map 21. Tel: 01606 737564.
LYME VIEW MARINA - Wood Lanes, Macclesfield Canal, Map 5. Tel: 01625 858176.
LYMM MARINA - Lymm, Bridgewater Canal, Map 15. Tel: 01925 752945.
MACCLESFIELD CANAL CENTRE - Macclesfield, Macclesfield Canal, Map 4. Tel: 01625 420042.
MAYORS - Tarleton, Rufford Arm, Leeds & Liverpool Canal, Map 31. Tel: 01772 812250.
NEW MILLS MARINA - New Mills, Peak Forest Canal, Map 7A. Tel: 01663 741310.
NORTHWICH MARINA - Northwich, Weaver Navigation, Map 32. Tel: 01606 44475.
ORCHARD MARINA - Rudheath, Trent & Mersey Canal, Map 20. Tel: 01606 42082.
PICKWELL & ARNOLD - Todmorden, Rochdale Canal, Map 41. Tel: 01706 812411.
PORTLAND BASIN MARINA - Ashton-under-Lyne, Peak Forest Canal, Map 9. Tel: 0161 330 3133.
PRESTON BROOK MARINA - Preston Brook, Bridgewater Canal, Map 17. Tel: 01928 719081.
WARBLE BOATBUILDERS - Hyde, Peak Forest Canal, Map 8. Tel: 0161 367 9205.
WINCHAM WHARF - Wincham Wharf, Lostock Gralam, Trent & Mersey Canal, Map 19. Tel: 01606 44672.

Lock furniture on the Weaver

How to Use the Maps

There are forty-six numbered maps whose layout is shown by the Route Planner inside the front cover. Maps 1 to 23 cover the main circuit of the Cheshire Ring, commencing at Hall Green, on the outskirts of Kidsgrove, and following the route of the ring in an anti-clockwise direction, via Marple, Manchester and Middlewich. Map 7A covers the Upper Peak Forest Canal to Whaley Bridge and Bugsworth Basins, whilst Map 17A covers the Bridgewater Canal to Runcorn. Maps 24 to 31 cover the route to Wigan and the Rufford Arm. Map 31A outlines the Ribble Link. Maps 32 to 35 cover the Weaver Navigation. Maps 36 to 43 cover the Rochdale Canal. The maps are easily read in either direction. The simplest way of progressing from map to map is to proceed to the next map numbered from the edge of the map you are on. Figures quoted at the top of each map refer to distance per map, locks per map and average cruising time. An alternative indication of timings from centre to centre can be found on the Route Planner. Obviously, cruising times vary with the nature of your boat and the number of crew, so quoted times should be taken only as an estimate. Neither do times quoted take into account any delays which might occur at lock flights in high season.

Using the Text

Each map is accompanied by a route commentary. Details of most settlements passed through are given alphabetically in the Gazetteer. Regular readers will already be familiar with our somewhat irreverent approach. But we 'tell it as we find it', in the belief that the users of this guide will find this attitude more valuable than a strict towing of the tourist publicity line.

Towpath Walking

The simplest way to go canal exploring is on foot. It costs largely nothing and you are free to concentrate on the passing scene; something that boaters are not always at liberty to do. The 'Cheshire Ring Canal Walk' was the first to be recognised as a long distance footpath in its own right, and whilst we, on our travels, have not seen much evidence of it being used as such, its towpaths are indisputably popular for walks of shorter duration. Over the years we have walked every yard of these ourselves, and they have been revisited to update this edition as thoroughly as possible. As usual the maps show the quality of the towpath, and whilst it does vary from area to area, none of it should prove problematical for walkers or cyclists.

Cycling

Cycling canal towpaths is an increasingly popular activity, but one which British Waterways - the body responsible for the upkeep of the bulk of Britain's navigable inland waterways - is only slowly coming to terms with. At present it is necessary for cyclists wishing to use towpaths to acquire a free of charge permit from a British Waterways office - see opposite page for appropriate addresses.

Boating

Boating on inland waterways is an established, though relatively small, facet of the UK holiday industry. There are over 30,000 privately owned boats registered on the canals, but in addition to these numerous firms offer boats for hire. These range from small operators with half a dozen boats to sizeable fleets run by companies with several bases.

Most hire craft have all the creature comforts you are likely to expect. In the excitement of planning a boating holiday you may give scant thought to the contents of your hire boat, but at the end of a hard day's boating such matters take on more significance, and a well equipped, comfortable boat, large enough to accommodate your crew with something to spare, can make the difference between a good holiday and an indifferent one.

Traditionally, hire boats are booked out by the week or fortnight, though many firms now offer more flexible short breaks or day boats. All reputable hire firms give newcomers tuition in boat handling and lock working, and first-timers soon find themselves adapting to the pace of things 'on the cut'.

Navigational Advice

LOCKS are part of the charm of canal cruising, but they are potentially dangerous environments for children, pets and careless adults. Use of them should be methodical and unhurried, whilst special care should be exercised in rain, frost and snow when slippery hazards abound. We lack space for detailed instructions on lock operation: trusting that if you own your own boat you will, by definition, already be experienced in canal cruising; whilst first-time hire boaters should be given tuition in the operation of locks before they set out.

Most of the locks included in this guide are of the standard narrow variety, but on the Rochdale Canal and on the Leeds & Liverpool Canal between Leigh and Tarleton and on the Ribble Link, they are widebeam and capable of accepting two narrow-boats side by side. The narrow locks on the Ashton flight (Map 10) and many of the locks on the Leeds & Liverpool and Rochdale are 'locked' to combat vandalism and a special 'handcuff' key is required to gain access to the paddle gear. These are obtainable from British Waterways offices and boatyards in the area. MOORING on the canals featured in this guide is per usual practice - ie on the towpath side, away from sharp bends, bridge-holes and narrows. An open bollard symbol represents visitor mooring sites, either as designated specifically by British Waterways or, in some cases, as recommended by our personal experience or that of our regular correspondents. Of course, one of the great joys of canal boating has always been the opportunity of mooring wherever (sensibly) you like. In recent years, however, it has become obvious that there are an increasing number of undesirable locations, particularly in urban areas, where mooring is not recommended for fear of vandalism, theft or abuse. CLOSURES (or 'stoppages' in canal parlance) traditionally occur on the inland waterways between November and April, during which time most of the heavy maintenance work is undertaken. Occasionally, however, an emergency stoppage, or perhaps water restriction, may be imposed at short notice, closing part of the route you intend to use. Up-to-date details are normally available from hire bases. Alternatively, British Waterways provide a recorded message for private boaters, the number to ring being: 01923 201401. Information is also available on BW's internet site at www.britishwaterways.co.uk

British Waterways

North West Waterways
Trafalgar House
Temple Court
Birchwood
Warrington
WA3 6GD
Tel: 01925 847700.

Wales & Border Counties Waterways
Navigation Road
Northwich
Cheshire
CW8 1BH
Tel: 01606 723800.

British Waterways operate a central emergency telephone service - Tel: 0800 4799947.

The Inland Waterways Association

The IWA was founded in 1946 to campaign for retention of the canal system. Many routes now open to pleasure boaters may not have been so but for this organisation. Membership details may be obtained from: Inland Waterways Association, PO Box 114, Rickmansworth WD3 1ZY.
Tel: 01923 711114 www.waterways.org.uk

Acknowledgements

Grateful thanks as ever to Brian Collings for the signwritten cover, his forty-first in the series; to Toby Bryant of CWS; to Karen Tanguy of Wayzgoose, to Tom & Tamar for their Manchester *pied-a-terre*; to Mike Webb of MSC; to Alan and Daniel Mawdsley of Fettlers Wharf Marina; and to Terry & Christine Rigden for boating facilities and home made cake on the Ribble Link and Weaver.

Thanks also to STIGE of Torino for their help and high standards in producing this volume - toto benne Giampiero, multo grazie!

Mapping reproduced by permission of Ordnance Survey (based mapping) on behalf of The Controller of Her Majesty's Staionery Office, Crown copyright 100033032

Information

BREAK FREE

Discover all Yorkshire's waterways
from our ideally situated base.
One way trips on all three Pennine
canals. Quality assured by VisitBritain.

Shire Cruisers
The Wharf
Sowerby Bridge
HX6 2AG
01422-832712
Fax: 839565
info@shirecruisers.co.uk
www.shirecruisers.co.uk

Boating holidays - moorings - all services